426 HEMI

America's Legendary Performance Cars

MUSCLE

RANDY LEFFINGWELL & DARWIN HOLMSTROM

PHOTOGRAPHY BY DAVID NEWHARDT

MOTORBOOKS

Dedication

For Randy Leffingwell, for not pigeonholing me as a motorcycle guy and letting me write about my first mechanical passion—muscle cars—and for my uncle David Grovum, who taught me not to believe everything I heard about cars and motorcycles. —Darwin Holmstrom.

For my friend, the late Jerry Sewell, who really loved these things, and who helped me to see them better. —Randy Leffingwell.

For my father, Clifford J Newhardt, whose style I have tried to carry on in everything I do. —David Newhardt.

First published in 2006 by Motorbooks, an imprint of MBI Publishing Company, Galtier Plaza, Suite 200, 380 Jackson Street, St. Paul, MN 55101-3885 USA

Copyright © 2006 by Randy Leffingwell, Darwin Holmstrom, and David Newhardt

MBI Publishing Company titles are also available at discounts in bulk quantity for industrial or sales-promotional use. For details write to Special Sales Manager at MBI Publishing Company, Galtier Plaza, Suite 200, 380 Jackson Street, St. Paul, MN 55101-3885 USA

ISBN-13: 978-0-7603- 2284-0
ISBN-10: 0-7603-2284-8

Editor: Peter Schletty
Designer: Mandy Iverson

Printed in China

On the front cover:
Pontiac kicked off the classic muscle-car era with its GTO. In 1969, the General Motors division introduced the outrageous Judge version of the car.

On the frontispiece:
Chevy offered SS versions of many of the divisions models, including the Monte Carlo luxury coupe.

On the title pages:
The 1970 GSX was one of the most well-balanced performance cars of the muscle-car era. It was available in either Saturn Yellow or Apollo White.

On the back cover:
Left: In 1969, Fred Gibb Chevrolet, a dealership in La Harpe, Illinois, commissioned the building of 50 Camaros with aluminum ZL-1 V-8s—cars known within Chevrolet as COPO 9560. Ultimately, Chevrolet built 69 of these outrageous machines.

Middle: In the spring of 2006 Dodge introduced the car muscle car enthusiasts have been waiting nearly four decades to buy: a new Hemi-powered Challenger.

Right: In January 1969 Mercury offered the Cale Yarborough Special, a version of its Cyclone Spoiler, as well as a Dan Gurney Special version of the same car. The identical cars differed only in their paint schemes, which were supposed to be Candy Apple Red and Wimbledon White for the Yarborough car and Presidential Blue and Wimbledon White for the Gurney car. Because dealers applied the Dan Gurney and Cale Yarborough decals, some white/blue cars appeared with Yarborough decals and some white/red cars appeared with Gurney decals.

CONTENTS

"Would you consider writing the foreword for our new American muscle car book?" asked authors Randy Leffingwell and Darwin Holmstrom, sheepishly. "Our photographer, Dave Newhardt, who just took some pictures of your '69 Judge, says you really know where the bodies are buried when it comes to the history of all these great cars."

Oh man…not another one! The last thing this world needs is yet another coffee table picture book about American muscle cars. On the other hand, these guys do have good reputations. They're not exactly novices on this subject. Maybe I ought to have a look before I say no!

Wow…what a surprise!

I'm going to start right out by saying, in my opinion, that this is the best study ever put together on the subject, and I ought to know—I was there. I stood right beside John DeLorean at the birth moment of the GTO and, as Pontiac's ad man, many give me credit for creating the mystique that surrounds America's first muscle car. From behind my desk as an automobile marketer, to being an active participant in the late night cruising scenes of the '60s and '70s, I witnessed this wonderful muscle car era, perhaps the greatest period in the entire history of the American auto industry.

So when I say, "These guys have done their homework," they have. Not only have they captured the facts, in both competent prose and glorious photos, but then they dug deeper. They not only tell you *what* each and every car was, complete with specs and photos, but they also tell you *why* each and every car was. What was the reason for its existence in the first place? Was it an industry trendsetter, a product breakthrough, or was it just another "me too" copy of a successful competitor?

This book presents not only a thorough product study, but also a thorough marketing study. No stone is left unturned. We get an intimate look at what America was all about, starting right after the end of World War II. We learn about "the boomers," you know, that fabulous mother lode of new car buyers who came into the marketplace, adolescents hungry not only for their first tastes of personal mobility on wheels, but on a set of *fast* wheels.

The authors start out with a discussion of the first really quick cars to show up after the war's end. The Olds Rocket, the great mid-fifties small-block Chevy, the Supercharged

Fords and, of course, the biggest bully of them all, the magnificent Chrysler Hemi. Then we get intimate with those fabled early NASCAR and NHRA Champions, the infamous 409 Chevy, the monster 421 from Pontiac, the 406 Ford, and those screaming sleepers from Mopar-land, the drag strip-dominating Max-Wedge Plymouths and Dodges.

Leffingwell and Holmstrom miss nothing as they take us inside the industry's bowels to witness the actual birth of the infamous muscle car. They are quick to tell you that this development was more than just the physical process of stuffing a big engine into a little car. Deftly written and with well-researched documentation, they trace the birth of every player, from the trendsetting Pontiac GTO through the hurry-up look-alikes from Olds, Chevy, Buick, Ford, Chrysler, and even humble little American Motors. They tell you how each one of these new horsepower and torque monsters quickly caught up and even surpassed the original state of the art. Was the 4-4-2 really stronger than the Goat? Would the 396, 375-horsepower, big-block Chevelle SS kick both of their tails? What about that Hemi GTX from Plymouth or a tough Gran Sport from Buick? And, to be kind, they don't overlook even the few 427 Fairlane GTAs from Ford.

They then go on to tell the inside stories about the creation of the fabulous pony cars, covering the early 271 Hi-Pos from Mustang and Cougar, all the way through the mighty rat-powered Camaros, Super-Duty Pontiac Trans Ams, 390 Javelins, and the living-breathing 440 and Hemi 'Cudas and Dodge Challengers. As readers, we struggle through the highs and lows of the performance world through the disappointing 1970s and '80s up to the beginning of the renaissance era of the 1990s and the new millennium. We visit intimately with the new generation of resurrected muscle cars that now include coupes, convertibles, 2-seat sports cars, 4-door sedans, station wagons, and even trucks.

Let me tell you folks, this is one great book. It's a story about America, its people, its culture, and its world-class cars. Not only is this yet another automobile coffee-table picture book—it's the *best one*.

Every reader will be able to say, "You know, I learned something today."

—Jim Wangers

Jim Wangers runs his 1969 GTO Judge through the gears.

As an advertising executive at MacManus, John & Adams, Pontiac's advertising agency, and as a national champion drag racer, Jim Wangers preached the gospel of high performance throughout the 1960s. His high-octane sermon inspired the development of Pontiac's GTO, the original muscle car, earning Wangers the title "Godfather of the Muscle Car."

THE IMMORTAL MUSCLE CAR

With 375 horsepower available from the L78 version of its 396-cubic-inch engine, no one could accuse the 1968 Chevelle of being underpowered. But in an era when buyers wanted the largest engines possible, 396 cubic inches seemed almost puny compared to the 428s and 440s offered by the competition.

N o other automotive experience matches the magic of executing a perfect second-third speed shift in a fast muscle car. For the most part, running a muscle car through the quarter-mile (even a perfectly tuned muscle car) is an exercise in brutality. It's exciting, thrilling even, and it's intense. But most of the time there's too much going on—too much car to control, too much power going to too little rubber, and too many parts that might break—to transcend the brutality of the moment and enter the magic zone.

When you drop the clutch and launch the car, you try to find a balance between wheelspin and traction, a delicate act when attempting to transmit outrageous torque through skinny, period-correct, bias-ply tires. When you make the first-second speed shift, wrestling oversized synchros around in that bone-crusher of a transmission, you're still doing the traction dance, trying to get the tires to hook up and blast you through the quarter-mile. By the time you make the final third-fourth speed shift, you're going fast enough for a muscle car's barn-door aerodynamics to come into play; the front end lightens up and steering inputs become more suggestions than direct controls. You're too busy trying to keep the beast on the road to truly enjoy the experience.

But a perfectly executed second-third speed shift is pure magic. You slam the gigantic shift lever up from second to third with no clumsy grinding noises emanating from the gearbox, then mash the right pedal to the floorboards while the rear wheels twist the engine's prodigious torque into the terra. At that moment you know what it feels like to wield God's own jackhammer, and you've experienced one of the peak moments in the automotive world. Muscle cars are loud, uncomfortable, and impractical compared to more sedate modes of transportation. But the moment you execute a perfect second-third speed shift you understand why people love them.

In post–World War II America, a bourgeoning youth population chose the automobile as a primary means of defining itself, and cruising American Main Streets became the activity of choice.

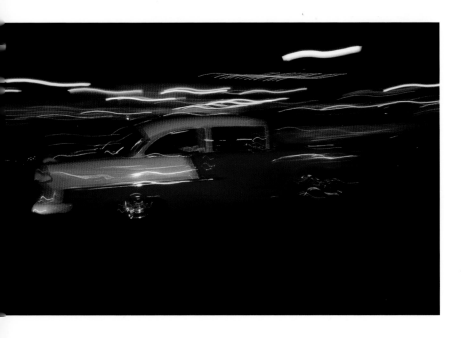

In the mid 1940s, Zora Arkus-Duntov, who eventually went on to engineer Corvettes for Chevrolet, and his brother Yura, developed the Ardun overhead-valve conversion kits for Ford flathead engines. These advanced pieces, which featured hemispherical combustion chambers, were made from heat-treated aluminum.

Chevrolet kicked off the big-block V-8 engine era when it introduced the 348-cubic-inch W-head in 1958. The hottest version of the engine produced 315 horsepower, making it one of the fastest engines on the market. But by the time this 1960 version hit the streets, the competition had developed even faster engines.

THE CLASSIC MUSCLE CAR ERA

Or at least you understand one of the reasons people love them. There's a lot more to the appeal of a muscle car than the act of driving one. A convertible Hemi 'Cuda didn't fetch $7.5 million in the spring of 2003 simply because the buyer wanted a fast car to run through the quarter-mile. A muscle car's appeal has as much to do with what it symbolizes as with what it actually is. Symbols are powerful things—people die for them every day—and a muscle car symbolizes freedom. More precisely, it symbolizes an era of freedom.

It was freedom that brought the muscle car into existence—the freedom of cheap gas and open roads, the freedom offered by the postwar American dream, the freedom to go just about anywhere and do just about anything. And it was the perceived loss of freedom that brought the classic muscle car era to an end. In the sour aftermath of the Vietnam War, the first war we clearly did not win, our sense of national omnipotence began to wither. With the loss of faith in our elected officials following the Watergate break-in, we suddenly found ourselves adrift without fixed stars to lead us into the future. After the shocking realization that oil was a finite resource, one that depended on forces beyond our control, we confronted the fact that the tap on our economy's lifeblood could be shut off at any time. The freedom symbolized by the muscle car suddenly seemed fragile and transitory in the face of this terrifying trifecta.

The classic muscle car era began when Pontiac introduced the GTO in 1964. This 1967 GTO convertible displays the so-called Coke-bottle styling that was trendy at the time (and still looks great today).

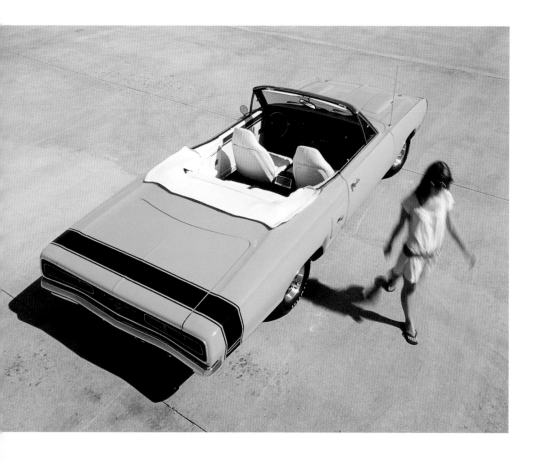

The classic muscle car era began in 1964 with the introduction of Pontiac's GTO. Earlier cars deserved the title "muscle car," to be certain, cars like Oldsmobile's 1950 88 coupe, the first sporty American car to offer an overhead-valve V-8 engine; Chrysler's 1955 C-300, with its 300-horsepower 331-cubic-inch Hemi engine; the fuel-injected 1957 Chevy; and Plymouth's 1963 Plymouth Savoy with its monstrous 426-cubic-inch Hemi. All of these cars are part of the muscle car story, but what distinguished the cars of the classic era was the confluence of the cars, the people who drove them, and the times in which the two came together. The people were the baby boomers, the huge generation born in the prosperous years after World War II. The time was the early 1960s, when the young people in the leading edge of the baby boom generation were coming of age, getting driver's licenses, and striking out on their own. The classic muscle car era began when Pontiac's chief engineer John Z. DeLorean and his team bolted a big-inch V-8 in an intermediate-sized car and marketed it specifically to this new tsunami of auto buyers.

General Motors limited its muscle cars to 400-cubic-inch engines in the late 1960s, but Chrysler operated under no such restraints. Chrysler offered the most potent engines for its muscle cars, including the 426-cubic-inch Hemi powering this 1970 Coronet R/T.

Pontiac unleashed the resulting GTO upon America at a time when the country's potential seemed unlimited. A marvelous system of highways opened up to endless possibilities. The network of two- and four-lane blacktop extending out beyond the horizon seemed as though it could take us anywhere we wanted to go, and the muscle car was the perfect vehicle to take us there. When those first lucky buyers cranked up the 360-horsepower Tri-Power 389 engines and drove their GTOs off dealer lots, they were heading toward something. They were taking their owners toward adventure, romance, success, the future. By the time the classic era ended, when the last buyer drove the last of Pontiac's Super Duty Trans Ams off a dealer's lot in 1974, he was more likely running away from something than running toward it. He may have been running from the encroaching nanny state that deemed his choice of transportation socially reprehensible, or he may have been running from the internal demons he brought home from the jungles of Vietnam. Given the tumultuous changes the United States had been through in the 10 short years since the birth of the GTO, he needed every one of those 455 cubic inches to outrun the chaos that seemed to be consuming society.

THE 400-HORSEPOWER TIME MACHINE

Before anyone realized what was happening, the muscle car was gone, replaced by baroque Monte Carlos, Cordobas swathed in yards and yards of fine Corinthian leather, and other landau-roofed "personal-luxury" cars. Gutless, gas-guzzling, smog motors strangled by ill-conceived, government-mandated pollution-control devices barely produced enough power to motivate their host vehicles up steep freeway entrance ramps. The word performance disappeared from the glossy brochures printed by auto manufacturers, replaced by words like crushed velour and landau top in an attempt to market these ponderous, lumbering cars. Performance would not return to the automotive lexicon for a generation.

Auto manufacturers responded to changes in society by changing cars, but in doing so they failed to take one important fact into account—though the conditions of our society had changed, its members hadn't. While the word performance had disappeared from

Since General Motors held muscle car engine displacement to 400 cubic inches, Oldsmobile made an end run around corporate management and went to George Hurst, owner of Hurst Performance Products, to build the 455-cubic-inch Hurst/Olds in 1968 and 1969.

Chrysler's Hemi engines have earned a mythic status in the pantheon of American performance cars, but the 440-cubic-inch RB engine was a much better choice for everyday driving. When equipped with the A12 Six Pack option—a trio of Holley two-barrel carburetors—this 390-horsepower monster could hold its own against a Hemi at the drag strip.

While some muscle cars handled fairly well, especially those built for Trans Am racing, no car could be called a legitimate muscle car if it couldn't burn through a quarter-mile in a cloud of tire smoke.

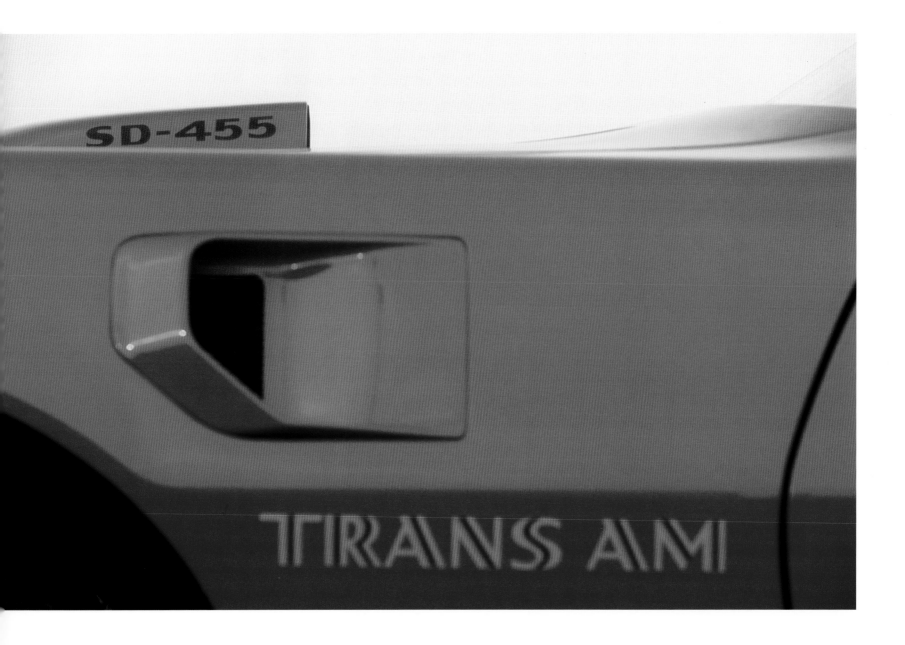

Pontiac kicked off the classic muscle car era with the original GTO, and brought the era to a close with the mighty SD455 Firebirds. Though only rated at 290 horsepower using SAE net measuring methods, the torque numbers told the real story. The SD455 produced 390 ft-lb of SAE net torque, the same SAE net number produced by the legendary 426 Hemi.

advertising copy, the need for speed hadn't diminished a bit. No one wanted a three-ton car propelled by a 145-horsepower boat anchor, and the American auto industry went into a tailspin. It wasn't until manufacturers made tentative baby steps back into the performance market in the mid-1980s that the industry began to recover. Auto industry bean counters might not be the sharpest blades on the Swiss Army knife of life, but they are smart enough to figure out that if some power is good, then more power is better, just as their predecessors had learned decades earlier. It wasn't long before Detroit once again became embroiled in a full-scale performance war.

Today we find ourselves in a new golden age of muscle cars. America's highways once again submit to the brute force of tarmac-rippling horsepower cranked out by such

Today we find ourselves in a second golden age of muscle cars. Cars like Ford's Shelby Cobra GT500 produce more horsepower and torque than any of the cars of the classic muscle car era.

legendary nameplates as "Mustang," "Corvette," "GTO," "Charger," and "Challenger." Engines bored out to 427 cubic inches and engines with hemispherical heads once again provide American muscle. But unlike their predecessors, today's muscle cars present the complete package—they stop and turn as well as go fast in a straight line, something that could never be said of a classic muscle car. A 2007 Shelby GT500 Mustang is as capable on a twisty racetrack as its street-racing ancestor, the 1965 GT350, and much more so than its original namesake, the 1967–1970 Shelby GT500. Perhaps what's most remarkable is that the new Shelby accomplishes all this without sacrificing comfort and convenience. In traffic it's as docile as a family sedan and as comfortable as any so-called personal luxury car.

It would seem that with such remarkable machines available at any modern dealership we would lose interest in the classic muscle cars, but that has not been the case. Even though today's muscle cars pound through the quarter-mile quicker than those of the classic muscle car era, and do so while coddling their drivers with comfort and convenience, we love the brutish muscle cars of the past now more than ever. That's because classic muscle cars can take us someplace the modern wonders only hint at: the past. ▮

Mulhollan
21300

CHAPTER 1
THE NEED FOR SPEED

5G 77 32

Since the beginning of automobiles, people have been trying to make their cars faster. One of the surest ways to do this is to decrease the weight by stripping off all superfluous parts—like fenders and bumpers.

21

Chevrolet set the mold for performance cars when it introduced its V-8-powered sedans in 1955. Anyone with a job could afford one of these powerful cars. By 1957, the fuel-injected V-8 engines, like the one powering this Bel Air, produced 283 horsepower—one pony per cubic inch.

Many people recall the post–World War II era as a simple time, and they are correct. It was a simple time, "simple" as in "uncomplicated," at least when compared to today. But it was also a simple time as in "unsophisticated." In hindsight the times were more unsophisticated than uncomplicated, because

in reality society underwent tremendous and complex changes during those supposedly placid years. The Soviets built an atomic bomb, people's lives were destroyed just because they'd gone to the wrong cocktail party, and the nation's youth seemed to be losing its collective mind, driven mad by listening to exotic rock-and-roll music.

During those years, when most people in the United States were exposed to television for the first time, dancing cigarette packages sold tobacco and sold it well; Arthur Godfrey and his ukulele achieved media superstardom; and the joke, "Take my wife . . . please," had the public in stitches.

By the mid-1940s, a V-8 was the engine of choice for anyone building a hot rod, but the only V-8 commonly available at the time was the Ford V-8, which used an antiquated side-valve design. Zora Arkus-Duntov and his brother Yura developed and sold Ardun cylinder heads to convert the side-valve engines to a more modern overhead valve configuration.

THE PIG IN THE PYTHON

Though postwar society appeared at once prudish and childish, its rampant sexual activity provided its most lasting legacy. Between the years 1946 and 1964, Americans had approximately 76 million children. As one postwar bride explained, "When my husband asked me if I wanted to go to sleep or what, I usually replied, 'Or what.'" The resulting rise in population reshaped society in much the same way that forcing a 4-inch piston through a 3-inch cylinder bore will reshape the 3-inch cylinder bore. This "baby boom" generation contained such a huge number of people that society had to bend around it rather than demand that baby boomers conform to society's mores. Hula-Hoops, tail fins, and Arthur Godfrey were transitory fads; the prodigious procreation of postwar Americans created a surplus of people that continues to reshape society today and will do so for decades to come.

Baby boomers certainly reshaped the automotive industry. The classic muscle car era—1964 to 1974—was Detroit's direct response to the market created by the indiscriminant genetic replication of the post–World War II generation.

To give credit where credit is due, the parents of the boomers began the process of transforming the auto industry even before they began the process of procreating the boomers themselves. When young men returned from the European and Pacific theaters of World War II, they came back restless, burning for something that polite society could not provide. They came back with a need for speed.

In his article "To Live and Die in Iraq," published in the August 2005 issue of *Vanity Fair*, author James Woolcott discusses the need for speed among returning war veterans. Woolcott writes:

> One psychiatrist attributed this daredevil driving to a testosterone infusion of invincibility feeding a need for speed in young men who dodged the Grim Reaper overseas and feel that nothing can harm them now—they've acquired *Survivor*-challenge immunity. So they buy "crotch-rocket" motorbikes and muscle cars and straighten out curved roads like Steve McQueen in *Bullitt* . . . .

In other words, vets returning from war today are having experiences not unlike the men who returned from Vietnam, Korea, or World War II. The main difference between the vets of today and the vets returning from World War II is that today's vets can walk into any auto or motorcycle dealership and satisfy their need for speed by simply writing a check for a high-performance car or motorcycle.

The situation in 1945 and 1946 differed vastly. At that time, the highest-performing stock motorcycle commonly available was the Harley-Davidson Knucklehead, which

In the 1940s, Ford's 1932 coupe became a popular platform from which to build a hot rod because the cars were cheap, light, plentiful, and had V-8s. Today these cars are still light and powerful, but are anything but cheap and plentiful.

cranked out a whopping 40 horsepower, and most passenger cars featured anemic inline sixes or flathead V-8s that produced less horsepower than most 600-cc motorcycle engines do today. Mounted in cars that weighed in on the heavy side of two tons, these engines produced less than stellar performance.

HOT RODS

But returning vets were resourceful. They'd been resourceful enough to dodge the very best that Germany, Japan, and Italy could throw at them, and they were resourceful enough to create fast vehicles from the parts at their disposal. The primary tools in their go-fast kit were bigger pistons and lighter weight.

Much of the modern speed technology we use even today was already developed and used in military applications during World War II. Many of the returning vets had flown planes with supercharged and turbocharged engines, but this technology wasn't readily available for civilian applications. Instead, speed demons in the late 1940s resorted to stuffing bigger engines in smaller vehicles. The biggest engine commonly available was a V-8, so that became the performance engine of choice. Chevy's reliable stovebolt six would do in a pinch, but for serious speed, a hot rodder wanted a Ford flathead V-8.

Not that a flathead engine was the best valve-train design for a fast engine. Its pair of valves feeding and emptying each cylinder resided below the combustion chamber, which sat off to the side of the cylinders, an inefficient design in regards to energy transferal. It was even worse from a thermodynamic standpoint. Flatheads ran hot. Heat sapped energy from the fuel charge and fatigued engine components to the point of failure, but there weren't a lot of options. Buick and Pontiac produced inline overhead-valve (OHV) eight-cylinder engines, but these were heavy, large, and not all that fast. They could be made to go fast, but they had a tendency to snap their extraordinarily long crankshafts in half when modified to produce too much power. Beginning in 1949, Cadillac and Oldsmobile began offering potent overhead-valve V-8s. These were the engines to have if you could afford them, but most hot rodders couldn't. Chrysler's and Chevrolet's overhead-valve V-8 engines would not debut until 1951 and 1955, respectively, leaving Ford's flathead V-8 and Chevy's stovebolt six as the most accessible options for postwar hot rodders.

The other tool in the hot rodder's kit was lighter weight. Young men had been stripping their cars of fenders and anything else deemed unnecessary to the pursuit of speed since before World War I, and they continued to excise as much superfluous sheet metal and equipment as possible in attempts to attain higher speeds.

There were a few modifications to be made to the Ford flathead at that time. A rudimentary aftermarket had sprung up before World War II. Popular speed equipment of the day included multiple-carb intake manifolds, steel-tube exhaust headers, and high-lift camshafts. After the war, a burgeoning speed industry began to flourish in Southern California. While the general population considered hot rodders sociopathic hoodlums, people like Vic Edelbrock Sr.

With its supercharger and Ardun overhead valve–conversion kit, this little deuce coupe produces enough power to run with the fastest cars from the classic muscle car era.

Because the cars offered by American manufacturers lacked the style that the emerging youth market craved after World War II, young hot rodders created their own style by modifying pre-war cars to suit their needs.
INSET: The cockpit of an early hot rod was all business—no subwoofers, pre-amps, DVD players, or PS2s here.

realized they offered a tremendous business opportunity. Edelbrock, an accomplished racer himself, began producing his Slingshot manifold in 1940 and selling it from his shop in Los Angeles. Before long a number of companies sprang up to service the hot rodders' need for speed.

The cars that served as platforms for the hot rodders' go-fast projects tended to be the least expensive and most commonly available cars: Fords, Chevrolets, and Plymouths. Being the most plentiful and usually the least expensive, Ford cars became the hot-rod starting point of choice. Model Ts and Model As were both plentiful and cheap. Better yet, Fords built from 1932 and on already had V-8 engines—affordable V-8 engines.

DRY LAKES RACERS, STREET RACERS, AND DRAG RACERS

By the 1920s hot rodders had begun racing their cars on the flat, hard-packed surfaces of California's dry lakebeds. For centuries torrential rainfall in the surrounding mountains had flooded into the basins of lakes in the Mojave Desert, like El Mirage, Muroc, Harper, and Rosamond. The water filled in imperfections in the sand, polishing the lakebeds

smooth. When the water evaporated, it left behind miles and miles of glassy-smooth, hard-packed lakebed, a perfect surface for running hot rods at high speeds.

Races in the dry lakebeds were anarchic affairs with a Brock Yates-esque "the-only-rule-is-that-there-are-no-rules" mentality. In 1938 a group of racers formed the Southern California Timing Association (SCTA). This group organized the racing into individual timed runs instead of the multicar free-for-alls that had been run in the past.

Not everyone had the resources to go to the dry lakes to race. Even though entry fees seldom exceeded $3, not everyone could afford $3. Nor could everyone make the difficult trip from Los Angeles to places like Muroc. The desert presented a brutal environment, and racers often spent race weekends sleeping under tarps, eating cold food, drinking warm beer, and fighting windblown sand. For many people, it was easier to simply find a lightly traveled stretch of public road and race on it.

By the late 1940s street racing had become a serious problem in Southern California. Organization had brought some measure of order and safety to dry lakes racing, so some far-sighted hot rodders made sporadic attempts to organize street racers. In 1949 a group of

After World War II, the growing number of young customers entering the automobile market wasn't satisfied with the cars Detroit manufacturers offered, which were too big and too slow for their tastes. Instead, they bought cheap cars and modified them to make them faster.

street racers met at Goleta Air Base near Santa Barbara, California, and competed in the first recorded organized drag race. The track was roughly a quarter-mile long, dictated not by some edict that it must be that length, but rather by the natural terrain. A small ridge in the runway approximately a quarter-mile from the starting line was chosen as the arbitrary ending point.

Organized drag racing got off to a slow start, but as dry lakes racing became increasingly specialized and increasingly expensive, the need for a more accessible form of racing grew. Drag strips sprang up around Southern California and surrounding states during the early 1950s. By 1952 there were six drag strips operating in Southern California. The sport had grown to the point where it needed a sanctioning body. In 1951 *Hot Rod* magazine editor Wally Parks formed the National Hot Rod Association (NHRA) and began organizing drag racing on a small scale. By 1955 the scale had become much larger, with the NHRA sanctioning 68 drag strips in 31 states. The organization had become the dominant force in drag racing, and continues to be so to this day.

The existence of the muscle car owes much to the existence of organized drag racing. While a handful of muscle cars have competed successfully on road racing courses—cars such as the Shelby GT350 and Boss 302 Mustang, the Z/28 Camaro, and the AAR 'Cuda and Challenger T/A twins, for example—drag racing has always been the muscle car's *raison d'être*. If a muscle car can corner like a kart, that's great, but it's just gravy. If it can't rocket through a quarter-mile strip faster than an ordinary sedan, it's not a muscle car. The requirements of drag racing drove the development of the American muscle car, and every aspect of the final product reflects the needs of the drag racer.

An industry devoted to making cars faster emerged prior to World War II, but options for high performance were still relatively limited in the 1940s. Speed freaks had been removing parts to lighten their cars since before World War I, and that was still the preferred means of achieving higher performance.

In addition to lighter weight, the other surefire method for making a car go faster was a bigger engine. In the 1940s, the biggest, most powerful engine commonly available was Ford's side-valve V-8.

HOT ROD AND THE ENTHUSIAST PRESS

Another critical factor in the development of the muscle car was the creation of the enthusiast press. One magazine in particular—*Hot Rod*—became the Bible for anyone interested in fast cars. Recalling the magazine's influence on his initial forays into engine modification, inveterate gearhead Jim Wangers wrote in his book *Glory Days*: "I didn't really know what I was doing, but if *Hot Rod* magazine said it worked, then I had to have it."

Robert E. Petersen and his friend Bob Lindsay cofounded *Hot Rod* magazine in 1947. The pair each coughed up $200 of their own money and printed 10,000 copies of the first issue. Petersen and Lindsay carried copies to local racetracks and drive-in restaurants around the Los Angeles area and sold them one copy at a time.

The automotive establishment was less than enthusiastic about their daring business venture. The American Automobile Association (AAA) considered Petersen, Lindsay, and anyone associated with the hot rod movement juvenile delinquents, all of whom should be locked away for the good of the country. When the magazine sponsored a car in the Indianapolis 500, officials tried to wipe the offending *Hot Rod* logo off the car.

Chrysler produced one of the first purpose-built performance cars from a major U.S. manufacturer in 1955: the Hemi-powered C-300.

Chrysler hired designer Virgil Exner to spice up its dowdy line of automobiles in 1949. In 1955, he produced his spiciest design yet—the C-300, which featured an early and subdued example of the tailfins that would soon grow to outlandish proportions.

While the C-300 was a performance car, it was a luxurious model aimed at an older, more affluent customer. Few younger buyers could afford the steep $4,110 price tag.

The checkered flag on the front badge of the C-300 wasn't just wishful thinking on some designer's part. The Hemi-powered Chryslers excelled in stock car racing.

But fans loved the magazine even more than the automobile establishment hated it. For the first time, car enthusiasts could learn the results from dry lakes and drag races without having to actually attend the events. Better yet, they could learn how to make their own cars faster. *Hot Rod* achieved tremendous regional success in its early years, and when editor Wally Parks formed the NHRA, that regional success translated to national success. The NHRA and *Hot Rod* magazine had a symbiotic relationship; the growth of one fueled the other, and soon both were major forces in the emerging youth culture.

The rise of the enthusiast press, particularly national magazines like *Hot Rod*, and later more mainstream magazines like *Car and Driver, CarCraft,* and *Motor Trend,* put in place another essential prerequisite for the creation of the muscle car. The explosion of media information outlets in the first half of the twentieth century—radio, television, specialty magazines—helped to unify the tastes and attitudes of the swell of young people entering society.

In addition to its sheer size, one of the defining attributes of the baby boom generation was its national homogeneity. The youth culture of the 1950s, 1960s, and 1970s differed from prewar generations in that it was a national culture and not a regional culture. Kids in Atlanta, Georgia, listened to the same music as kids from Portland, Oregon. Kids in Albuquerque, New Mexico, watched the same television programs as kids in Ithaca, New York. And kids from Pittsburgh, Pennsylvania, read the same car magazines as kids in San Diego, California. The styles and trends among young people in one part of the country moved in lockstep with those from every other part of the country, and the need for speed became a national, rather than local, phenomenon.

DETROIT JOINS THE PARTY

The younger generation's need for speed did not pass unnoticed by the country's major automakers. Astute members of Chrysler, GM, and Ford management teams picked up on the sea change in the auto-buying public's taste. They didn't quite understand the nature of the change they were witnessing—a coming cultural revolution fueled by a massive growth in the youth population—and they didn't quite understand how to capitalize on those changes. For the most part they continued to produce the same family-friendly sedans they had always produced. But they did understand at least one important thing: Their customers wanted more power.

Detroit didn't initially start producing faster cars as a direct response to the needs of the young men spreading the hot-rod gospel around the country. Mounting more powerful engines in postwar cars made practical sense. Cars were growing bigger, a necessary evil if they were to be roomy enough to transport the large number of children that were being born. They were also becoming more luxurious, providing owners with an increasing list of creature comforts like power steering, power brakes, and automatic transmissions, conveniences that sapped power from already overtaxed engines. Cars needed more powerful engines just to preserve the performance status quo.

The easiest path to more power was to build engines with more cylinders, and in the late 1940s other manufacturers began to follow Ford's lead and build V-8 engines. But unlike the Ford, which still used the antiquated flathead design in its V-8 power plants, other manufacturers developed more modern combustion chamber designs.

The heart of the C-300 was its 300-horsepower, dual-four-barrel V-8 engine with hemispherical combustion chambers. This first-generation Hemi featured a true hemispherical—or dome-shaped—combustion chamber, rather than a semi-hemispherical shape, as found on the later 426-cubic-inch Hemis of the 1960s and early 1970s.

Ford designer Frank Hershey had the benefit of two model years of Corvette sales figures to draw upon when Ford introduced the 1955 two-seat Thunderbird. Lackluster Corvette sales led Hershey to guess—rightly—that Americans wanted a personal luxury car like the T-Bird rather than a pure sports car like the Corvette.

By the late 1940s the V-8 engine had a long history among U.S. automakers. Cadillac offered the first production V-8 in an American car in 1914, and Henry Ford introduced his V-8 engine in 1932, but as noted above, that engine was an archaic flathead that produced just 65 horsepower in its original form. Something more modern would be needed to power America's cars into the brave new postwar world. In 1949 Cadillac and Oldsmobile both responded to that need, offering the American market its first mass-produced overhead-valve V-8 engines. Oldsmobile's 303-cubic-inch Rocket 88 V-8 produced 135 horsepower and the Cadillac OHV a whopping (for the day) 160 horsepower. In 1951 Chrysler upped the ante.

ENTER THE HEMI

The Chrysler Hemi engine came about as a direct result of World War II, when Chrysler engineers experimented with hemispherical combustion chambers in an attempt to extract greater power from tank and aircraft engines. The hemispherical combustion chamber was not a new idea. In 1904 the Welch passenger car featured a four-cylinder engine with hemispherical heads. Offenhauser race engines used hemi heads, as did Stutz, Duesenberg, and Miller automobiles. Hemispherical—or dome-shaped—combustion chambers provided the most possible volume from a given surface area, leading to a very efficient design. When Chrysler began developing a V-8 engine for its passenger cars in the postwar years, the hemi design was a logical choice.

Chrysler introduced the new V-8 in its top-of-the-line 1951 models: the Saratoga, New Yorker, Imperial, and Crown Imperial. These cars may have looked frumpy and old-fashioned, but with the new 331-cubic-inch V-8 cranking out 180 horsepower—20 more than its nearest competitor, the Cadillac OHV V-8—Chrysler could lay claim to producing Detroit's hottest engine.

By 1955 a redesigned Chrysler Hemi put out 300 horsepower when fed by a pair of dual four-barrel carburetors. It was time for Chrysler to mount the engine in a car with some style. In 1949 Chrysler had hired Virgil Exner, one of Detroit's top auto designers to

To power its new two-seater, Ford used its new overhead valve Y-block V-8, which replaced the antiquated side-valve design in 1953.

Although Spartan by today's standards, the Thunderbird's cockpit was a luxurious place to spend time in 1955.

Buyers of a 1955 Thunderbird had the choice of an automatic transmission or a three-speed manual, shown here. A four-speed manual transmission was not offered.

take the frumpiness out of its cars, and by the time Chrysler unveiled the legendary C-300, Exner had succeeded in doing just that. The C-300 was long, low, sleek, and fast; it was most definitely a muscle car.

Unfortunately the C-300 lacked one of the most important components of a successful muscle car: an affordable price. In 1955 the C-300 sold for a steep $4,110. This put the car out of reach of all but the most well-heeled hot rodders. Chrysler had most of the formula for a successful muscle car down already—a powerful engine in a sporty body—but the youth market would have to wait a bit longer for affordable Mopar muscle.

SUPERCHARGED 1957 THUNDERBIRD "F-BIRD"

With one notable exception to be discussed at great length in later chapters, Ford's postwar history is one of not quite connecting with the youth market. The company has produced some spectacular cars, but often those cars have not quite shuffled to the same beat as the majority of automotive enthusiasts.

This was true from the earliest days of Detroit's involvement in the post–World War II performance-car battles. Even though the Ford Motor Company's products formed the backbone of the early hot-rod movement, its showroom offerings in the late 1940s and early 1950s seemed a bit peculiar to younger car buyers. For example, while Dodge, Plymouth, and Chevrolet were marketing high-performance six-passenger sedans to younger customers, Ford introduced a sporty two-seater that was neither sedan nor sports car: the Thunderbird.

Designer Frank Hershey and his team conceived the Thunderbird as a direct competitor to Chevrolet's upcoming Corvette, a pure sports car, but Hershey and company developed a car that could more accurately be described as the prototypical personal luxury car. This was intentional. Debuting the Thunderbird for model year 1955, two model years after Chevrolet introduced its two-seat sports car, Ford had the advantage of one year's worth of customer reaction to study. American customers differed from European auto enthusiasts—Americans wanted comfort and convenience, even if that came at the expense of weight and handling. Thus, most Thunderbirds sported every luxury feature Ford offered: electric windows, power steering, power brakes, power seats, automatic transmissions, and radios.

Ford's interpretation of a sporty American two-seater proved to be much more to the liking of the buying public than Chevrolet's purist sports car. Ford sold 16,155

Thunderbirds in 1955 compared to just 700 Corvettes sold that year. The lesson learned? Give the American public convenience or suffer sales death on the showroom floor.

To compensate for the heft added by all this convenience, an overhead-valve V-8 powered the new Thunderbird. This engine, dubbed the Y-block, represented Ford's final abandonment of the archaic flathead design which had been produced until 1953. The new OHV 292-cubic-inch power plant generated 193 peak horsepower at 4,400 rpm, and 280 ft-lb of torque at 2,500 rpm when mated to a manual transmission. To compensate for the increased mechanical drag imposed by the optional automatic transmission, Ford engineers bumped the compression from 8.1:1 to 8.5:1, providing 5 more ponies and 5 additional ft-lb of torque.

The Y-block provided more than adequate motivation for the Thunderbird, but more than adequate was no longer enough for the American buying public. Its appetite had been whetted for more of everything, including horsepower. In 1956 Ford responded by taking the boring bar to the Y-block and punching out the holes, in this case creating 312 cubic inches of displacement. This optional engine produced 215 horsepower with a manual transmission and 225 horsepower with an automatic. For those wanting even more power, Ford offered what it called the "Super V-8," a 312-cubic-inch mill topped by dual-four-barrel carburetors that bumped power to 260 ponies.

With the 1957 Thunderbird, Ford produced one of *the* classic designs in automotive history.

INSET: The vents on the front quarter panels of the 1955 Thunderbird are non-functional. Hershey's stylists origianlly designed functional louvers on the front quarter panels, but the chief engineer, concerned about exhaust fumes entering the cockpit, had them blocked off.

The top engine option for the 1957 Thunderbird was a 312-cubic-inch V-8 featuring a McCulloch single-stage, centrifugal-type supercharger. Dubbed the F engine, the supercharged T-Bird cranked out 300 horsepower.

Although the 260-horse 312 provided exceptional performance, customers inevitably wanted more. For 1957 the dual-four-barrel version of the 312 Super V-8, dubbed the E engine, cranked out 270 horsepower in street trim. Even so, the E engine no longer occupied the top spot in the Thunderbird's engine hierarchy. In 1957 Ford also offered an F version of the 312. Although this engine featured just one Holley four-barrel carburetor in place of the E engine's pair, that carburetor breathed through a McCulloch single-stage, centrifugal-type supercharger. In street trim, the blown 312 produced 300 horsepower, but there was much more power available for the clever tuner to unleash.

With the F model, Ford had produced a 3,000-pound rocket, a genuine muscle car, but one that failed to connect with the buying public. Ford sold just 211 of these magnificent machines. Perhaps supercharging was an idea too far ahead of its time in 1957, but that is only part of the reason the Thunderbird failed to connect with the burgeoning youth market. The fact that the car only had room for the driver and a passenger likely played a larger role, since sales rose to 37,892 units in 1958, the year the Thunderbird sprouted two additional seats. (This was the 1950s, remember, and dating either was chaperoned, or couples went together on double dates. A single guy showing up at the front door in a two-seater to pick up his girlfriend often met her father, an encounter that frequently changed the evening plans.) Four-seat Thunderbird sales represented a 16,000-unit increase over 1957's output, in spite of the fact that the country was in recession in 1958.

1957 marked the last year of the two-seat Thunderbirds; in 1958 the T-Bird sprouted rear seats and sales skyrocketed.

While the original two-seat Thunderbirds were undoubtedly high-performance cars, they were too expensive, too exotic, and too exclusive to develop much of a following among younger car buyers.

Yet even with four seats, the Thunderbird never really connected with the youth market. Even in its early years as a two-seater the car had a stately, elegant presence, one that seemed incongruous with the cars that dominated the classic muscle car era. Still, there's no denying the fact that the F Bird had the cajones needed to run with the best Detroit had to offer back in its day.

FUEL-INJECTED 1957 CHEVROLET

Chevrolet had greater success reaching a younger market with its performance offerings than did either Ford or Chrysler. Although not the first on the scene with a V-8, Chevrolet was the first to bring a truly affordable overhead-valve V-8 engine to the masses. In the fall of 1954 Chevy unveiled a new line of cars it called the "Motoramic Chevrolets." Originally Chevrolet downplayed the new engine in its ad copy, touting the car's comfort, convenience,

and styling instead of its performance, but anyone who knew anything about hot-rodding cars knew that the new V-8 was an engine with significant performance potential. Called the Turbo-Fire V-8, the new engine's specifications don't seem especially impressive today—265 cubic inches capped by a two-barrel carburetor and producing only 162 horsepower, a little more than half that of Chrysler's top-of-the-line Hemi—but savvy buyers at the time knew they were looking at something special. Anyone who had struggled to generate power from a Ford flathead V-8 knew that Chevy's overhead-valve design, with its stamped, lightweight rocker arms and no rocker shafts, gave the engine potential to produce many more horses.

Chevrolet engineers immediately began mining the new engine's potential, developing a "Power Pack" option consisting of a four-barrel carb and a dual-exhaust system that bumped horsepower to 180. With this car, Chevrolet hit the mark. Performance enthusiasts recognized the bang for the buck offered by the new Chevy Super Turbo-Fire V-8s and

With the 1957 Chevrolet, General Motors' Bowtie division produced one of the most iconic American cars of all time. The Chevrolets of this era set the pattern for American performance cars for generations to come.

One of the most striking aspects of the 1955–1957 Chevrolet design was its relatively compact dimensions. In overall length, width, and curb weight, these cars were closer to the muscle cars of the following decade than they were to the full-sized sedans produced during the 1960s and 1970s.

took the cars straight from the showrooms to the racetracks. The Chevrolets dominated their classes at Daytona Speed Week in 1955. Privately entered Chevrolets (Chevy didn't officially participate in racing at this time) won the top four spots in the acceleration tests measured from a standing mile. Chevys won the top two spots in the under-$2,500 class, three of the top five spots in the two-way measured mile event, and first place in the 100-mile event on the short half-mile track. The only car that was consistently faster that week was Chrysler's C-300, which cost almost twice as much as the Chevrolet.

Shrewd people like Jim Wangers at Campbell-Ewald, Chevrolet's advertising agency, recognized what such racing success could do to Chevrolet sales. A hot rodder himself, Wangers knew what excited younger customers, and he convinced Campbell-Ewald and Chevrolet to capitalize on this success. Another essential component of the muscle car genetic code had been set in place: marketing campaigns aimed at stirring excitement among young males.

The sales success of the Power-Pack option led Chevrolet's brain trust to the sensible conclusion that more power would result in even more sales. For 1956 they upgraded the

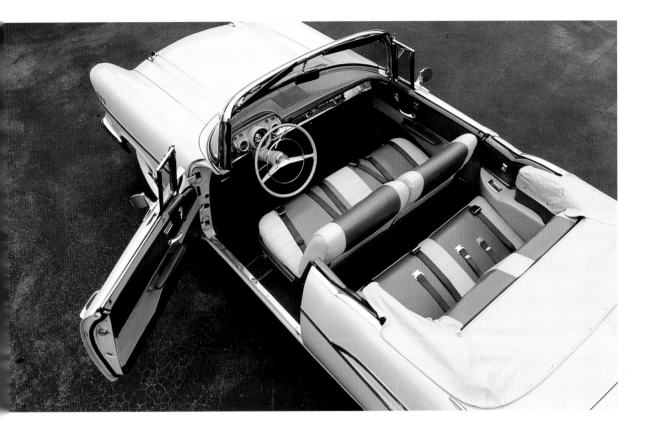

The Chevrolets of the mid-1950s struck a perfect balance between luxury, affordability, and performance.

Super Turbo-Fire engine to 205 horsepower. The 1956 Chevy with a Power Pack was an inexpensive, stylish car that could barrel through the quarter-mile in 16.6 seconds, making it one of the strongest performing cars a person could buy. By that time, every half-bright gearhead had figured out that there was a lot more potential performance lurking beneath the hood of the "Hot Ones," as the advertising copy called the V-8 Chevrolets. Chevy's own engineers proved this when they released an even-more-super version of the Super Turbo Fire, this one featuring a pair of four-barrel carbs forcing their fuel charge through valves operated by solid lifters. This engine produced 225 horsepower. A special edition of the Super Turbo Fire V-8 used Duntov camshafts, bumping horsepower to 240, making it Chevy's strongest mill yet.

But Chevy's whiz-kid engineers weren't about to stop at 240 horsepower. In 1957 they produced the most radical power plant ever to darken an American auto's engine bay: a 283-cubic-inch V-8 fed by a Rochester Ramjet fuel-injection unit. Chevrolet had been experimenting with fuel injection since

When Chevrolet introduced the 283-horsepower fuel-injected version of its small-block 283-cubic-inch V-8 in 1957, it achieved an engineering milestone: one horsepower per cubic inch.

Thanks to its 283-cubic-inch, 283-horsepower, fuel-injected small-block V-8, this 1957 Chevrolet Bel Air convertible can use every bit of its 120-mile-per-hour speedometer.

The era of the tailfin was in full swing by the time Chevrolet introduced its 1957 models.

the early 1950s and made the results of their work available to the public for the 1957 model year. The injection unit consisted of a two-piece cast-aluminum manifold incorporating tuned ram tubes running to the intake ports. Air- and fuel-metering equipment mounted on the side of the lower casting measured and injected air into the intake plenum just ahead of the intake valves. Individual nozzles metered fuel into each eylinder. Though this system proved to be a bit finicky and difficult to start, it pushed power output to true muscle car levels. With hydraulic lifters, the "fuelie" produced 250 horsepower. When fitted with solid lifters and pop-up 10.5:1 pistons, power jumped to 283 horses, achieving a long hoped-for industry and enthusiast goal of one horsepower per cubic inch in an American production engine.

Though it turned Chevrolet's sedans into high-powered street fighters, the fuel-injected engine proved too complex, too finicky, and too expensive for regular passenger-car use. After 1959, it was only offered in the Corvette.

With the fuel-injected 1957 Chevy, GM had almost perfected the muscle car formula. The car was fast, stylish, and though the fuel-injection option was relatively expensive, the total price of the car was still a bargain when one considered the level of performance. But the fuelie proved to be a case of too much too soon. The fuel-injection system was a bit too complicated for the technology of the day, and people just weren't ready for such complexity. Nor were they ready for the system's $484.25 price tag. With the exception of the exotic Corvette, Chevrolet stopped offering passenger cars with fuel injection after the 1959 model year.

Ford, GM, and Chrysler all made noble attempts to serve the youth market in the 1950s, and to varying degrees all three major U.S. auto manufacturers enjoyed success with their sporty offerings, but the best was still to come. The baby boomers were still preteens when U.S. automakers made their first tentative steps into the performance car market. These companies were just learning the craft of marketing to young people. About the time they would perfect that craft in the following decade, there would be a waiting market of young car buyers, the size of which would astound the corporate bean counters of the 1950s. ∎

Chevrolet capitalized on the racing success of its V-8-powered cars by placing checkered-flag logos on every available surface.

CHAPTER 2

BETTER LIVING THROUGH HORSEPOWER

Chevrolet's 348-cubic-inch W-head engine—the original big-block—powers this 1960 Chevrolet Biscayne. By 1960, the ubiquitous tail fins had become passé and stylists were experimenting with new looks, such as horizontal fins instead of the tall vertical versions of the late 1950s.

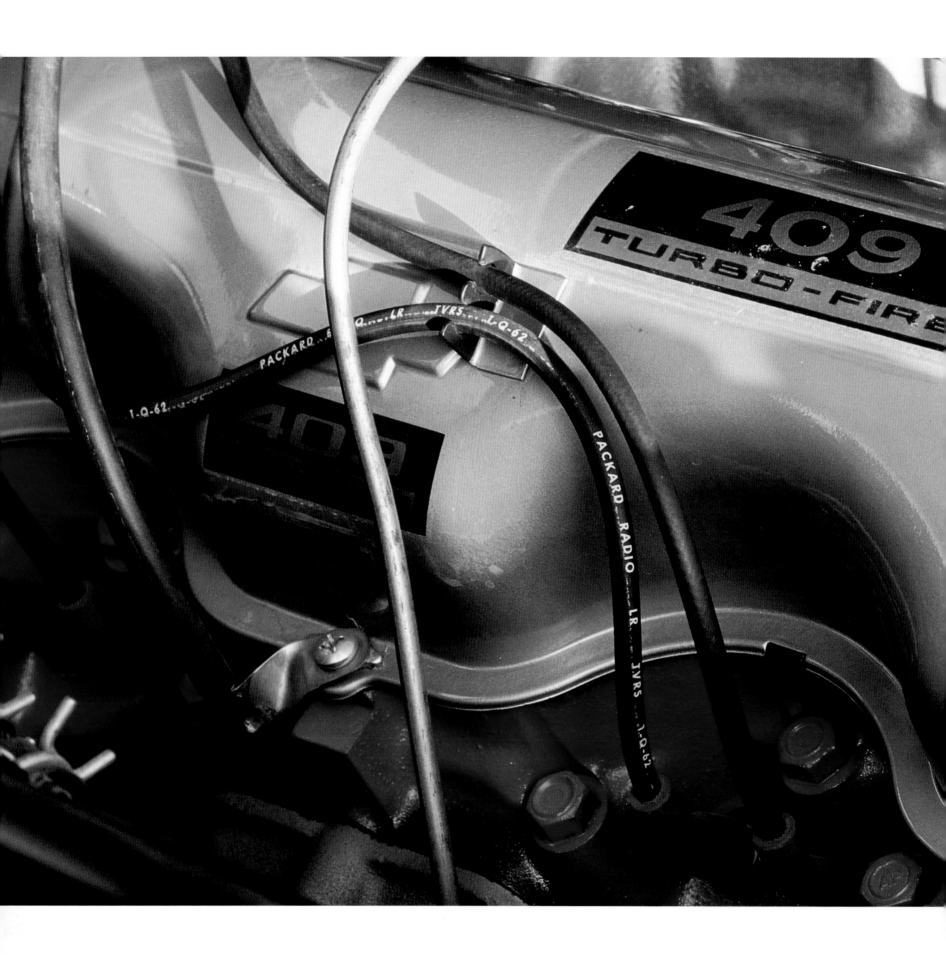

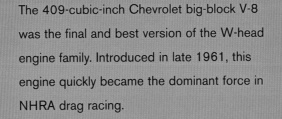

The 409-cubic-inch Chevrolet big-block V-8 was the final and best version of the W-head engine family. Introduced in late 1961, this engine quickly became the dominant force in NHRA drag racing.

C hevrolet introduced its small-block V-8 just when America needed the kind of excitement a fast, affordable car could provide. With the end of the Korean War, the country had entered an extended period of peace and prosperity, one with no apparent end in sight. The United States found itself in a cold war with the Soviet Union, a situation that lent an underlying

sense of dread to day-to-day life, but it was an abstract dread with little direct effect on the comings and goings of most citizens. For the most part, optimistic exuberance fueled the American psyche, exuberance reflected in the automotive industry. During the late 1950s and early 1960s, Detroit experienced a period of technological explosion, a period in which the automotive industry's best engineers perfected the overhead-valve V-8 engine. During this time the small-block V-8 gave way to the big-block V-8, another element needed to bring the muscle car to iconic status.

The fuel-injected, small-block V-8 disappeared from the sedans' option list by 1960, and designers toned down the styling, eliminating some of the excesses of the 1959 models.

Muscle car technology entered the scene well before the advent of the classic muscle car era. Even though Chevrolet had developed what would become the prototype for the muscle car—a reasonably priced stylish sedan with big V-8 power—the market still needed to undergo a few changes before the time would be right for the classic muscle car era to commence in earnest. Primarily, the baby boom generation needed to age a few more years before it would become the 8,000-pound gorilla of the car-buying public. As the

1950s gave way to the 1960s, most boomers were still more interested in Schwinn bicycles than Detroit muscle; it was their parents who were buying most of the new cars.

The boomers hadn't started buying cars of their own yet, but the youth market grew increasingly larger throughout the 1950s. Even in this prehistory of marketing and demographic research, carmakers noted the growing number of young buyers entering the market each year. The auto manufacturers recognized the potential sales such buyers represented and began developing cars that met the needs and desires of these young drivers. Apparently they desired power and needed speed, as witnessed by the growing popularity of racing.

The competitive atmosphere of the drag strip held a natural attraction for the burgeoning population of young people coming of age in the late 1950s and early 1960s. After the tumult and chaos of the first half of the twentieth century, with its seemingly endless wars and police actions, most mature adults were ready for a period of relative calm. But the younger generation that came of age during the late 1950s and early 1960s hadn't

In 1960 and 1961, Chevrolet offered a version of the 348 W-head big-block engine topped by three two-barrel carburetors and producing 350 horsepower.

Pontiac began offering its Super Duty line of high-performance parts for its cars in 1959. By 1961, Super Duty Pontiacs like this Catalina dominated NHRA drag strips and cleaned up on NASCAR super speedways.

experienced the first two World Wars and the Great Depression, and this generation was genetically predisposed to racing fast cars.

The human animal appears to be hard-wired for adventure and excitement, a feature that made us particularly adept at hunting for mammoth meat and running away from saber-toothed tigers. In periods of peace and prosperity we get very little chance to exercise the fight-or-flight instincts that make us suited for such work. It seems that in periods in which life is relatively easy we manufacture the danger and excitement needed to

appease those instincts. In such times a large portion of the population re-creates scenarios that provide excitement and danger; we place ourselves in situations that bring out those instincts. When we no longer needed to kill wild animals for survival, we began killing them for sport. When we are not risking our lives in combat, we risk them on the freeways during our daily commute.

Some people seem to possess a thrill-seeking gene that makes this instinctive response even stronger. These people, usually males young enough to lack a sense of their own mortality, take things one step further. They create danger by jumping out of airplanes, diving to the ocean's floor, and racing their cars in organized competition. As the 1950s ended, this population found its numbers increasing exponentially.

While the baby boom generation hadn't entered the automobile market at the dawn of the 1960s, their influence was already felt. If Pontiacs were beating Chevrolets at the local drag strip, these speed-obsessed youngsters were likely to lobby their parents to purchase a Pontiac instead of a Chevrolet.

Pontiac considered itself an upscale brand when compared to corporate rival Chevrolet, and the interior of Pontiacs always exuded a luxurious feel. This remained the case throughout the classic muscle car era.

Part of Pontiac's success at the drag strip can be attributed to the cars' basic designs. The long, rear overhangs meant that more of the cars weight was placed over the rear wheels, giving them better traction when taking off.

If you wanted a Super Duty engine in your 1961 Pontiac, you had to build it yourself with Super Duty parts purchased from your Pontiac parts counter. Installing Super Duty parts meant you would likely be the terror of the local drag strip, but it also meant that you instantly voided your car's warranty.

RACING AS A MARKETING TOOL

The fascination younger customers had with speed and racing did not escape the attention of corporations that wanted to market their products to this affluent new generation. The auto manufacturers took particular interest in stock car racing and drag racing because racers competed in stock-bodied cars in both forms of racing. Without question a Chevy, Plymouth, or Pontiac winning on a NASCAR (National Association for Stock Car Auto Racing) oval track or an NHRA drag strip inspired some buyers to purchase a similar car from a Chevy, Plymouth, or Pontiac dealership and, to varying degrees, manufacturers embraced these forms of racing.

Certain elements within the upper echelon of the auto industry hierarchy felt uncomfortable with such a sordid activity as racing, regardless of its marketing potential. A growing federal government occasionally glanced toward the auto industry when cautious voters complained about speed and accidents. In 1957 the Automobile Manufacturers Association (AMA), at the time the primary lobbying group of American auto manufacturers, instituted a voluntary ban on factory involvement in racing in an effort to turn away government scrutiny. While all manufacturers paid lip service to this ban, most simply made an end run around it and continued to be involved in racing in a more covert fashion. Chevrolet's and Pontiac's clever ways of working around the ban provided the most brazen examples of back-door factory racing support, with factory engineers and technicians themselves competing on the weekends. Ford, on the other hand, followed the ban almost to the letter. This slavish adherence to such a misguided policy put Ford at a disadvantage when the muscle car wars began to heat up, a disadvantage from which Ford never completely recovered.

Drag racing proved to be an exceptionally effective way of building brand image, because it was the most accessible form of racing, especially with the 1957 introduction of the NHRA Super Stock class, in which stock-bodied cars competed. The NHRA had experienced phenomenal growth during its first decade. In 1957 the organization held its first national event, called the Nationals, in Great Bend, Kansas. The NHRA held the Nationals at different drag strips around the country each year before finding a permanent home in Indianapolis. In 1961 the NHRA added a second national event, the Winternationals in Pamona, California. Drag strips became a nexus where an entire generation of young motorsports enthusiasts came together to compete against one another. More often than not they raced each other in the same cars they drove to work during the week, running them in the Super Stock class. They'd drive to the track, bolt on a set of Atlas Bucron tires, drop the exhaust pipe, and go racing.

Automakers had a vested interest in seeing their cars winning in this class. A young man was much more likely to plunk his hard-earned money down on a car that won at the drag strip than on one that lost. Even if the kids attending the races were too young to buy cars of their own, their influence on the cars their parents purchased was increasing. If Chevrolets were beating Pontiacs at the drag strips, kids were lobbying their parents to buy Chevys instead of Pontiacs. This was a generation of people whose parents seemed to indulge their every whim. Their parents had been cheated of a proper childhood because of economic depression and war; they wanted to make their children's experience of childhood a happy one. If the kids wanted dad to buy a Chevy instead of a Pontiac, there was a good chance he'd buy a Chevy.

To acknowledge its status as General Motors' performance division, Pontiac offered optional racing equipment, like tachometers, in most of its models.

In January 1961 Chevrolet introduced the ultimate version of its W-head big-block V-8: the 409. By the time this 1962 Bel Air hit the streets, the 409 had already become a street-racing legend.

BIRTH OF THE BIG-BLOCK

If a Chevrolet whipped a Pontiac on the drag strip, it meant that Chevys would whip Pontiacs on the sales charts. Thus, it was in each manufacturer's best interest to develop cars that would whip the cars built by the other manufacturers, and with the then-current technology, the surest path to success was excess. The late 1950s saw most auto manufacturers developing big-inch engines with which to pummel their competition into submission.

Since introducing its revolutionary small-block V-8, Chevrolet had perfected the combination of affordability and power, but with its fuel-injected small-block of 1957, Chevy had pushed the outer limits of both. In 1958 the company decided to substitute brute force for high technology and introduced a larger big-block V-8. Dubbed the W-head, this new engine shared no parts with the small-block V-8. Originally displacing 348 cubic inches, this physically massive engine had the potential to be bored out to a much greater displacement.

In stock trim, with a single four-barrel carburetor, the new big-block cranked out a mere 250 horsepower, but there was much more power available. When ordered with three two-barrel carburetors, a high-lift cam with mechanical lifters, and an 11.0:1 compression ratio, the engine produced 315 horsepower. An increase in compression ratio the following year pumped horsepower up to 335.

With this engine General Motors had created another important piece of the muscle car puzzle: the big-block engine. While there would be many overachieving small-blocks in the muscle car pantheon, the archetype for American muscle has always been a two-door sedan powered by a monster big-block engine—the bigger and more monstrous, the better. The big-block engine is the reason a perfectly nice Challenger convertible powered by a 318-cubic-inch engine will never be worth more than a fraction of the value of an original Hemi 'Cuda, even though the small-block engine makes much more sense in a street car that will never see the business end of a drag strip.

If your car's front fender didn't read "409" in 1962, you might as well have been driving a Rambler.

The skinny bias-ply tires with which Chevrolet equipped its cars in 1962 didn't stand a chance against the massive 409 ft-lb of torque produced by a 409.

SUPER DUTY

Intracorporate rivalry between Chevrolet and Pontiac meant that Chevy could count on Pontiac to respond to its new big-block engine, but the enthusiasts running Pontiac weren't content with simply aping Chevrolet's "bigger-is-better" philosophy. Pontiac didn't need to develop a new big-block engine, since the V-8 their division introduced in 1955 was more than up to the task. In fact, that engine block formed the basis of every Pontiac V-8 of the classic muscle car era.

When introduced in 1955, the engine displaced just 287 cubic inches, but engineers had left plenty of room to punch out increasingly bigger holes, which they proceeded to do each year. In 1956 they bored it to 316 cubic inches. In 1957 they took it to 347 cubic inches, and in 1958 to 370 cubic inches. The following year they punched it out to 389 cubic inches, a capacity that would soon prove to be significant. That year they also introduced a monstrous 421-cubic-inch version of the engine. By not developing separate small-block and big-block engines, but rather developing a single versatile engine design, Pontiac engineers had created a highly adaptable platform. This adaptability would be advantageous once the muscle car era began in earnest.

Pontiac not only provided a versatile engine capable of winning races, it found the most creative ways to circumvent the AMA ban on factory racing involvement as well. A band of mavericks ran the Pontiac division: General Manager Semon E. "Bunkie" Knudsen and Chief Engineer Pete Estes, along with the man who would later succeed both of them, John Z. DeLorean. These men understood the relationship between racing success and brand image better than any other people in the auto industry, probably because they were all racing enthusiasts themselves.

The team had solid raw material from which to build performance cars. In 1959 Pontiac capitalized on the potential of its engine by offering its Super Duty line of high-performance components. Even though the AMA banned factory involvement in racing, a buyer could transform his Pontiac into a full-blown factory drag racer by ordering Super Duty parts. Pontiac had been supplying high performance parts to buyers for years, but the parts had come from other manufacturers and not Pontiac. Bunkie Knudsen wanted the parts designed and built in-house to keep the profits generated within the Pontiac division, so he created a special group within

Chevrolet shrank its sedans in 1961, and eliminated the tail fins altogether. In 1962, designers cleaned up the lines of the Chevy's cars even more.

Four-speed transmissions were obligatory for any car with drag racing potential by 1962, as were tachometers. No one ever wrote a song about a 409 equipped with an automatic.

For 1962, the 409 engine was substantially upgraded with a recast block, improved heads with larger valves, and a higher compression ratio. Sales of Chevy's biggest big block increased dramatically, from a mere 142 409s sold in 1961 to nearly 15,000 sold in 1962.

The 1962 Chrysler sedans were the last designed by Virgil Exner. By this time Exner's lines were no longer in step with the buying public's taste, and cars like this Belvedere traded on the strength of their potent engines rather than their looks.

The 413-cubic-inch Max Wedge engines were the most powerful factory engines of the early 1960s, producing 420 horsepower.

Pontiac's engineering department: the Super Duty Group. This was, of course, the equivalent to Knudsen thrusting his middle finger at the AMA. In his book *Glory Days*, Jim Wangers, by then an account executive at MacManus, John & Adams, Pontiac's advertising agency, quotes Knudsen as saying, "'If those guys want to be fools and withdraw from racing, let them. But I've got a car to save and I haven't got time to be a gentleman. We're going racing.'"

The Super Duty Group's goal was to develop a package of engine parts that would withstand the stress of racing. Every Super Duty–equipped Pontiac had the parts to do that, starting with a stout engine block with four-bolt main bearing caps. Forged crankshafts, connecting rods, and high-compression pistons meant that an owner could expect many reliable trips through the quarter-mile traps between engine rebuilds. Tri-Power carburetors (Pontiac's branding of its triple two-barrel setup) pumped a huge fuel charge through a high-flow aluminum intake manifold and into special big-valve heads, and the spent fuel charge exited the combustion chamber via high-flow header-type exhaust manifolds.

This was serious equipment, clearly intended for racing competition and not for street use. (Super Duty parts carried no factory warranty.) The radical profiles of the cam lobes meant that at low rpm the solid lifters would pound the finish right off the surface of the cams, not a desirable trait in a vehicle that has to idle at a traffic light. Driving Super Duty–equipped cars as intended also led to problems; after cleaning the tires and blasting down the drag strip, the engines produced enough heat to melt the aluminum intake manifolds, necessitating a cool-down period before driving back to the pits. When Pontiac specified Super Duty parts "for racing purposes only," it wasn't joking.

Pontiac not only violated the AMA ban by selling cars equipped with parts "for racing purposes only," it violated the ban by racing those cars. Jim Wangers developed a relationship with Royal Pontiac, a Pontiac dealer in the Detroit suburb of Royal Oak, a relationship that led to a national drag racing championship. In 1960 Wangers drove a Super Duty–equipped Royal Pontiac to victory in the Super Stock class at the NHRA Nationals, with a best quarter-mile performance of 13.89 seconds at 102 miles per hour.

Applying Exner's curvaceous, organic lines to the squared-off shapes common on sedans in the early 1960s led to oddly styled cars.

Though their dowdy looks made the 1962 Chryslers seem old-fashioned, they were technologically-advanced cars, with unit-body construction and torsion-bar suspensions.

NOTHING CAN CATCH HER

By the early 1960s, Chevrolet's 348-cubic-inch big-block didn't look so big any more. Even Ford, a company that embraced the AMA ban on factory racing involvement, offered a 390-cubic-inch big-block engine that saw success on drag strips and stock car oval tracks around the country. Chevrolet needed to respond, and respond it did, in the form of a W-head engine punched out to 409 cubic inches. Introduced late in the 1961 model year, this stroked-and-bored engine provided inspirational performance.

While Chrysler's styling was out of tune with public tastes, its decision to downsize sedans contributed almost as much to the drag racing success of its cars as the potent Max Wedge engines did.

A push-button automatic may seem a strange choice for a car intended for drag racing, but in 1962, Chrysler didn't offer a proper four-speed. Besides, the A-727 Torqueflite automatic introduced in 1962 was an excellent racing transmission.

For 1963, Chrysler engineers punched out the cylinder bores of the Max Wedge engine to create a 426-cubic-inch, 425-horsepower monster that dominated NHRA drag racing.

In base four-barrel form the new 409 produced 360 horsepower and a massive 409 ft-lb of torque. Mounted in the engine bay of the stunning new Super Sport Impala Sport Coupe, a base 409 with proper gearing could run through the quarter-mile traps in under 15 seconds. With a little tuning, the right tires, and some proper performance parts, the new engine was capable of much better times than that. The new 409 quickly became a dominant force in NHRA drag racing, and Don Nicholson won the Stock Eliminator class at the 1961 NHRA Winternationals.

The basic design of the car helped transfer the engine's prodigious torque into the tarmac. Like its Pontiac cousin, Chevy's coupes featured long rear overhangs, placing a large portion of the cars' weight directly over the rear wheels. This helped the tires hook up during quarter-mile runs and led to improved trap times.

Chevrolet's success on the nation's drag strips led to sales success, just as it had done for Pontiac. When something can be proven numerically and the performance-equals-sales

equation works, even the bean counters running General Motors can figure it out. The logical conclusion was that if a lot of power equaled strong sales, then even more power would equal more sales, so for 1962 the 409 received a performance makeover. Power output of the base four-barrel version jumped to 380 horsepower, thanks to redesigned cylinder heads with larger valves, redesigned pistons and combustion chambers, and a redesigned intake manifold. The hot version of the engine received a pair of four-barrel carburetors—the famous "dual-quads" in the Beach Boys' song "409." So equipped, the "four-speed, dual-quad, Posi-Traction 409" cranked out 409 horsepower—again a Chevy engine generated one pony per cubic inch—and could run the quarter-mile in the high 12-second range with very little tweaking.

Ford engineers increased the displacement of its FE-series big-block V-8 to 390 cubic inches in 1961. With three two-barrel carburetors, solid lifters, and a dual-point distributor, the engine produced a respectable 401 horsepower.

When Robert McNamara departed Ford Motor Company in early 1961, he took his philosophy of no fun with him and Ford was once again in the business of building high-performance cars like this 1962 Galaxie 500.

INSET: Though Ford had developed a potent big-block engine by 1962, its cars never achieved much success in NHRA drag racing; they were too big and too heavy to compete against competitors like the downsized Chryslers and Chevrolets.

MOPAR'S MAX WEDGE

When Chevy introduced its new big-block in 1958, it shocked the other auto manufacturers into action, and soon most U.S. automakers were promoting the performance potential of their cars. Chrysler, which had long prided itself on building the ultimate performance V-8 engines, found the fact that humble Chevrolet now offered one of the most powerful automobiles on the market especially galling. Chrysler engineers had taken the aging Hemi engine about as far as they could by this point, and in 1958 they countered Chevy's big-block with a new big-block engine of their own: the "wedge" B-block engine. Because development money was too tight to design different engines for each of its brands—Chrysler, Dodge, Plymouth, DeSoto—the company used this new engine across its entire product line. To disguise the fact that the same mill that powered a mighty Chrysler 300 also motivated a lowly Plymouth, each brand offered the new V-8 with slightly different displacements ranging up to 361 cubic inches.

The new B engine would prove to be one of Chrysler's best and longest-lived engine designs. Distinguished by its deep-skirted block and front-mounted distributor, the power plant earned the nickname "wedge" because its combustion chambers were wedge-shaped rather than hemispherical (dome-shaped) or polyspherical (double-dome shaped), as were earlier Chrysler V-8 engines. Wedge technology more closely adhered to the orthodox thinking of the day.

Topped off by a pair of four-barrel carburetors, the 361-cubic-inch wedge cranked out 320 horsepower, five more than Chevrolet's hottest big-block. Chrysler offered an even more powerful version, one fed by a Bendix electronic fuel-injection system, producing 333 horsepower, but that system was an unmitigated disaster. While Chevrolet's Rochester mechanical fuel injection was difficult and finicky, the Chrysler system was impossible and few remained in operation for very long, rendering the dual four-barrel-equipped version of the B-block the top performer.

Chrysler engineers knew Chevrolet would increase the power output of its new big-block, so in 1961 they punched out the cylinder bore of their new wedge engine, mounting the most powerful version in the company's premiere performance car, the 300. When equipped with a pair of Carter AFB carburetors feeding the combustion chambers through a pair of aluminum 30-inch Cross-Ram intake manifolds, the 413-cubic-inch version of this engine produced 400 horsepower, 100 more horsepower than the Hemi engine that powered the original Chrysler 300-C of 1955.

The top 406-cubic-inch FE-series big-block V-8 had been tuned to produce 405 horsepower by 1962. Unfortunately for Ford, Chevrolet had tuned the top version of its 409-cubic-inch engine to produce 409 horsepower that same year.

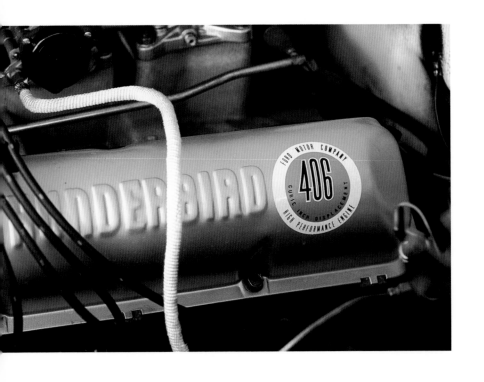

Like General Motors, Ford offered a four-speed transmission for its high-performance cars, but it wasn't enough to help the big, heavy Galaxies achieve much success in NHRA drag racing.

Chrysler marketing folks saw the results Chevrolet and Pontiac were achieving at drag strips around the country. More importantly, they saw the effect Chevrolet and Pontiac sales success was having on Chrysler's corporate bottom line—people who bought Chevrolets and Pontiacs weren't buying Dodges and Plymouths. The company needed to sell more cars to earn more money, and to sell more cars it would have to go racing. The problem was its luxurious 300s and Furys and Polaras were too big and too heavy to make good drag racing platforms. The company needed a radical solution to this problem, and the solution it devised was radical by any definition of the word. In 1962 Chrysler mounted its B-block engine in its new, smaller-sized B-body cars. These were still full-sized cars and not intermediates, but they were smaller and lighter than the cars offered by GM and especially Ford.

Chrysler engineers didn't mount garden-variety B-block engines in these smaller cars; they used high-performance engines designed strictly for drag racing. This engine, officially called the "Ramcharger" when mounted in the Dodge chassis and the "Golden Commando" when mounted in the Plymouth, but unofficially called the "Max Wedge," featured radical solid-lifter camshafts, large-port heads, and dual Carter AFB carburetors mounted atop a short ram intake manifold. In its most powerful form, this engine package produced 420 horsepower, making the new lightweight Chrysler products the belles of the drag strip ball. Pontiac had dominated drag racing in 1960. In 1961, Chevy's hot 409 had been the car to beat. In 1962, Mopars became the force to be reckoned with, and would remain so for a very long time.

ROBERT MCNAMARA AND THE PHILOSOPHY OF NO FUN

Even though Ford had been building modern overhead-valve V-8 engines since the mid-1950s, it had never managed to recapture the performance image it had earned with its flathead V-8 engines. Robert McNamara, who had joined Ford as manager of planning in 1946 and had worked his way up through the ranks to (briefly) become the first president of the company not named Ford, lacked any passion for performance cars. He believed cars should be used for transportation rather than something as frivolous as having fun, and he embraced the AMA ban on factory racing involvement. To create his ideal vision of pure proletarian transportation, McNamara oversaw the creation of the Ford Falcon econocar.

In January 1961, less than five weeks after assuming the presidency of Ford Motor Company, McNamara took his "no-fun" philosophy to Washington, D.C., where he would orchestrate U.S. military affairs as John F. Kennedy's, and later Lyndon B. Johnson's, secretary of defense. This would prove disastrous for the U.S. military, but worked to Ford's advantage.

In 1963, Ford replaced the 406 with a 425-cubic-inch version of the FE-series big-block V-8, which it called the 427, in reference to NASCAR's 427-cubic-inch upper-engine displacement limit. Galaxie 500s with the new 427 dominated NASCAR racing in 1963, winning 23 Grand National events.

Like its sister Ford division, Mercury built a performance car using the FE-series big-block V-8—the Marauder.

In 1962, Pontiac made its 421-cubic-inch Super Duty engine available as a factory option in its Catalina and Grand Prix models to keep the cars eligible for NASCAR competition. NASCAR had instituted a rule that effectively banned the use of over-the-counter Super Duty parts on its super speedways.

McNamara's midlife career change put Ford back in the business of building cars that people wanted to buy. Unfortunately, the competition had a six-year head start on Ford, another disadvantage from which Ford would never fully recover.

Ford had the basics to build a solid performance car. Like Chevrolet, Ford had developed a big-block V-8 engine, the FE series, introduced in 1958. With a top displacement of 352 cubic inches and a peak output of 300 horsepower, the FE big-block didn't set the drag racing world on fire, though a special Thunderbird powered by a 430-cubic-inch version of the FE engine won the first NASCAR race at Daytona in 1959. In 1961, the year of McNamara's departure, Ford engineers took a boring bar to the block and punched out the engine displacement to 390 cubic inches. With three two-barrel carburetors, solid lifters, and a dual-point distributor, the engine produced a respectable 401 horsepower. Another overbore in 1962 raised the power output of the new 406-cubic-inch engine to 405 ponies.

When Chrysler replaced the 426 Max Wedge engine with the 426 Hemi in 1964, the company never intended the engine for use in a street car, although a small number of the outrageous powerplants found their way into road-going cars, like this Dodge Super Stock.

This put Ford's big-block engine in the hunt and Ford-powered cars had some drag racing success, but the cars from GM and Chrysler still dominated the sport. The main problem with Ford's offering was the weight of Ford's full-sized sedan, the Galaxie. The Galaxie, especially the Galaxie fastback, originally designed for NASCAR racing, was a handsomely styled and comfortable car, but even the special lightweight version developed for the drag strip weighed 100 to 150 pounds more than its competition from GM and Chrysler. Combined with a horsepower rating that was probably optimistic (if anything, the GM and Chrysler engines put out more power than advertised) this excess weight relegated Ford to also-ran status in the drag racing wars of the early 1960s.

One of the few clues as to the madness that lurked in this car's engine bay was the upside-down shovel of a hood scoop, which fed fresh air to the omnipotent 426 Hemi below.

THE BILL FRANCE CONNECTION

The drag strip might have been the primary venue in which manufacturers could showcase the performance of their automobiles, but stock car racing also provided a high-profile stage upon which to promote performance cars. The premier stock car racing organization, then as now, was NASCAR. Formed in 1948 at a time when there were still very few new cars on the road—civilian production was still ramping up following the end of World War II—NASCAR originally consisted of races between highly modified cars that bore little resemblance to those sold to consumers. In 1949 NASCAR president Bill France Sr. decided that fans would prefer to watch races between cars based on the same ones they drove on the street—actual stock cars—and he was right. Once NASCAR began featuring the same Hudsons, Oldsmobiles, Pontiacs, and Plymouths that transported fans to the races, its popularity began to grow.

Not only did the switch to stock cars make NASCAR more popular with fans, it made the sport more popular with auto manufacturers. Detroit began producing increasingly powerful engines to propel their cars to NASCAR winner's circles. In many ways, NASCAR racing drove V-8 engine development even more than did drag racing.

By the late 1950s, Pontiacs performed extremely well in NASCAR racing, thanks to Division Manager Bunkie Knudsen's blatant disregard for the 1957 AMA ban on racing. Pontiac's Super Duty line of performance parts meant that a racer could purchase anything he needed to build a competitive stock car from the same dealership that sold

KEEP VALVES CLOSED
WHEN ENGINE IS STOPPED

ALWAYS CLOSE NEEDLE VALVES
BEFORE SWITCHING FROM ONE
FUEL TO ANOTHER • WHEN BOTH
VALVES ARE OPEN AT ONE TIME
THE FUELS WILL MIX • THIS
MAKES IT IMPOSSIBLE TO START

PRINTED IN U.S.A.

him the car. But these parts were only available over the parts counter. A buyer couldn't order a car straight from the factory equipped with Super Duty parts. He had to buy the parts separately and install them himself, instantly voiding the car's warranty. This policy also helped to appease the AMA and deflect government scrutiny. Knudsen and others regularly commented to reporters and legislators that they could not stop their customers from buying parts and modifying the cars they had purchased.

Super Duty Pontiacs ruled NASCAR tracks by the early 1960s, winning 30 Grand National races and the manufacturer's championship in 1961. To keep one brand from dominating the sport, NASCAR instituted a rule that would have a significant impact on the classic muscle car era—it required manufacturers to sell passenger cars with the same engines it raced. This meant that the over-the-counter Super Duty parts Pontiac sold would no longer be eligible for NASCAR competition, so in 1962 Pontiac made its 421-cubic-inch Super Duty engine available as an option in its Catalina and Grand Prix

Original owner Lynn Ferguson ordered this car with a 426-cubic-inch Max Wedge. Because the Max Wedge had gone out of production when Ferguson ordered the car in January 1964, Chrysler substituted with its new Hemi racing engine.

models. For the first time, a buyer could buy a Super Duty Pontiac without having to assemble it himself. In 1962, Pontiac won its second manufacturer's championship.

Chevrolet didn't fare as well in NASCAR racing. While its 409 dominated the nation's drag strips, the W-head big-block engine used an antiquated combustion chamber design that made it poorly suited for the extended high-speed running required of a successful NASCAR racer. Not that the Chevys performed poorly in NASCAR. Chevrolets won 14 Grand National races in 1962 and placed second in the manufacturer's championship behind Pontiac.

But Chevrolet was not content to play second fiddle to Pontiac. For 1963 it introduced a new big-block V-8: the Mark II. With a more modern combustion-chamber-in-head design (the combustion chamber in the 409 had been in the block), the new engine featured all the hot-rod tricks of the day: lightweight valvetrain, header-style exhaust manifolds, and dual-plane aluminum high-rise intake manifolds. Chevrolet's new big-block displaced 427 cubic inches, placing it right at the displacement limit allowed by NASCAR. Racing journalists and other racers referred to the new power plant as the "mystery engine," because Chevrolet erected security barriers around the garages at Daytona to prevent anyone from seeing it up close.

THE GENERAL MOTORS RACING BAN

The mystery surrounding the engine did not lead to racing success for Chevrolet, but not because of any technical details of the engine. Chevrolet, as well as Pontiac and the other GM divisions, faltered in NASCAR racing because in 1963 General Motors instituted a total ban on factory racing involvement. Ed Cole, the father of Chevrolet's OHV V-8 engine and by that time a vice president at General Motors corporate headquarters, decided to halt all corporate racing activities, both direct and indirect. A former manager of GM's Chevrolet division, and its chief engineer before that, Cole knew all the tricks people like Bunkie Knudsen used to circumvent the AMA racing ban of 1957 and he was determined to stop them. In late 1962, GM announced that the company would cease all support of racing for 1963.

Cole had a reason for this madness. Unlike McNamara, Cole didn't feel it was his personal duty to end all forms of automotive fun, and he wasn't hell-bent on promoting a nanny state in which government and the corporate world contrived to protect automotive enthusiasts from themselves. In fact, Cole instituted the total racing ban in an attempt to ward off the intrusive arm of the nanny state; by the early 1960s, GM had the federal government breathing down its corporate neck.

"This wasn't due to safety concerns or emission problems," Jim Wangers writes in *Glory Days*. "That would come later in the decade. The heat was from the Justice Department, who had determined that GM was getting too large a share of the U.S. car

market." The real problem was that General Motors had come dangerously close to breaking the Sherman Antitrust Act of 1890, the federal antitrust law designed to prevent one company from monopolizing an entire industry.

"You have to understand," Wangers says, "in the late '50s, early '60s, GM was in danger of getting between 57 and 60 percent of the new car market. The Justice Department said they were watching GM, and if GM ever got to 60 percent of the market or more, they'd move in and break up the company. They'd done it before with Standard Oil, so we knew they were serious. General Motors took the posture to take actions to slow down market penetration. That's why [Cole] issued the edict to ban racing in 1962. They got rid of multiple carburetors. They even went so far as to withhold cars from the enthusiast press."

In 1964, all the Hemi sedans Chrysler produced were two-door posts (with the exception of Lynn Ferguson's hardtop). This car was one of a dozen lightweight versions that had had their steel bodies dipped in acid to dissolve away metal for lightness.

ONE WORD: HEMI

Eternally the number three American automaker, Chrysler found itself in no danger of being on the stinky end of the federal government's trust-busting stick. The company wanted as large a market share as it could get, and if racing success equaled increased market share, then Chrysler Corporation would do everything in its power to ensure racing success—even if it meant bringing an elephant to a cockfight. That elephant took the form of a reborn Hemi.

It's not that Chrysler vehicles had been under-armed in the performance wars prior to the rebirth of the Hemi. The company's Max Wedge engine used every hot-rodding trick to dominate America's drag strips. The Max Wedge had been bored out to 426 cubic inches beginning June 1, 1963, just slipping under NHRA's limit of 427.2 cubic inches for Super Stock engines. Its parts list summarized the state of pushrod V-8 engineering art: double-row timing chain, one-piece short-ram aluminum intake manifold topped by a pair of four-barrel carburetors, header-type exhaust manifold, high-capacity fuel pump, dual-point distributor, forged-aluminum pistons, Magnafluxed connecting rods, high-strength valve spring retainers, smaller crankshaft pulley to limit belt speeds, heavy-duty clutch with an aluminum clutch housing. It even had a deep-sump oil pan that was baffled to prevent oil from sloshing away from the sump when the car inevitably wheelied off the starting line. No one accused Chrysler's B series big-block of being underpowered. With an optional 13.5:1 compression ratio, the engine produced 425 horsepower, enough to earn Chrysler-powered cars four NHRA records in 1962.

Like Chevy's 409 before it, Chrysler's Max Wedge ruled American drag strips but didn't fare as well on NASCAR oval tracks. Chrysler president Lynn Townsend had two sons who were performance-car enthusiasts, so he knew how important racing success was to his company's image. Townsend knew that to compete in an increasingly youth-oriented market, Chrysler would have to succeed in NASCAR as well as in drag racing. Townsend asked Bob Hoover, head of Chrysler's race engine group, what it would take for Chrysler to win Grand National races. In his book *Hemi: The Ultimate American V-8*, author Robert Genat quotes Hoover's response: "'If you want to go there and go like stink, let's adapt the Hemi head to the race B engine.'"

The conversion proved no simple task. Chrysler engineers needed to design stronger connecting rods to support the massive Hemi pistons and the entire head had to be rotated inward toward the engine to provide clearance for the exhaust pushrods to clear the head gaskets.

Chrysler's 426 Hemi engine revolutionized motorsports in America. Although rated at the same 425 horsepower as its Max Wedge predecessor, true output topped 500 ponies, and when mounted in lightweight drag racing specials, the new power plant dominated the drag strip. The basic design continues to win races in the Top Fuel and Funny Car classes well into the twenty-first century.

More importantly, the engine decimated the competition on NASCAR's superspeedways. Debuting at the 1964 Daytona 500, Hemi-powered Mopars took all three spots on that year's Daytona podium. Richard Petty, who stood atop the Daytona 500 podium that year, went on to win the 1964 Grand National championship.

The lightweight Hemi-powered cars were good—exceedingly good—at one thing, and one thing only: transporting their owners down a quarter-mile-long strip of asphalt in the shortest time possible.

Because factories developed increasingly specialized drag racing cars like the 1962 Chevrolet Z-11 Impala, the NHRA instituted the Factory Experimental, or F/X, class to keep the factories from dominating the popular Super Stock classes.

FACTORY SPECIALS

Two racing rule changes would have dramatic aftershocks in the consumer car market. The first was NASCAR's homologation rule requiring NASCAR race cars to use only engines available in passenger cars sold to the public. The other was the NHRA's creation of the F/X (Factory Experimental) class, in which highly modified cars powered by special low-production engines would compete.

In part, this new class represented an attempt by the NHRA to keep the factories from dominating drag racing. The average drag racer could not hope to compete against the low-volume drag racing specials coming out of Detroit. Built with exotic lightweight materials like aluminum and fiberglass, these cars included the legendary Z-11 Impala, Super Duty Pontiacs, lightweight Galaxies, and Super Stock Dodges. Detroit produced these cars in such low volume that they were all but unattainable for the average drag racer. For example, Chevrolet built just 57 Z-11s and Ford built just 11 of the lightweight Galaxies.

General Motors' ban on factory racing involvement proved another factor driving the creation of the F/X class. General Motors announced the ban late in 1962, after Pontiac

had already delivered a number of 1963-model Super Duty drag racing cars to customers. Because these cars would not be offered as production cars in 1963, they didn't qualify for the Super Stock class. By creating the F/X class, the NHRA created a venue in which the owners of these cars could compete.

NASCAR's homologation rules meant that manufacturers would have to mount their sophisticated new V-8 engines in at least 500 passenger cars if they hoped to campaign them on America's superspeedways. Chrysler would have to build street-going cars equipped with the firm's all-conquering Hemi. Chevy would have to offer customers cars powered by the new Mark II big-block engine, and Ford would have to mount the radical new versions of its FE engines in the engine bays of cars meant for public roads. If manufacturers wanted to campaign cars in the highly competitive Super Stock class, they would have to build wickedly fast street cars. In 1964, a horsepower war was about to erupt onto America's streets and highways, a war that would be fought with machines that exceeded all expectations of even the most demented car enthusiast. ▦

Ford built the Thunderbolt, a special drag racing version of the Fairlane, in 1964. It featured fiberglass fenders and Plexiglas windows to save weight, and a 427 engine tuned to crank out an estimated 500 horsepower.

CHAPTER 3
MARKETING MUSCLE

The 1966 Hurst GeeTO Tiger was conceived by Jim Wangers, George Hurst, and Petersen Publishing to cross-promote the GTO, Hurst products, and various Tiger-based marketing programs at Pontiac.

Most of the mechanical development of the pushrod V-8 had already taken place at the dawn of the classic muscle car era in 1964. Throughout the period, no regular production engine surpassed the brute performance of the mighty 426 Hemi, though a few matched it.

The creation of Chrysler's 426 Hemi marked the end of a period of intense engine development and the beginning of a period of intense marketing. With the Hemi, the pushrod overhead-valve V-8 engine reached a technological pinnacle. In just 15 years the OHV V-8 design had evolved from Oldsmobile's 135-horsepower Rocket 88 into a fire-breathing 500-horsepower monster.

If development had continued at that pace, today's small-block Chevy engine would generate over 10,000 horsepower, and in the early 1960s it looked as if development might just continue at that pace indefinitely.

In reality, the pushrod V-8 engine had been taken just about as far as was possible by 1964. The basic mechanical architecture had been developed almost to perfection; future developments would focus on electronic controls, first with electronic ignition and later with space-age engine management computers. "A big failing of the cars of the muscle car era was a lack of ignition," Jim Wangers says today. "In low-speed running, the spark

Monza Sport Sedan—one of 7 new models in the Corsa, Monza and Corvair 500 series for '65.

Beautiful Shape for '65—CORVAIR
If this one doesn't knock you right off your chair,
we can't imagine what would

It took one of the most dramatic car changes ever made to bring you this new beauty with the international look. Here, briefly, are some of the wonderful things we've done to the 1965 Corvair.

First, there's racy new hardtop styling on every Corvair Sport Coupe and Sport Sedan—even the lowest priced ones.

And all are longer and lower than Corvairs of old, yet with curved side windows to give you more shoulder room inside.

The steering is even quicker, too. The ride is steadier with its new 4-wheel independent suspension. The brakes are bigger. The wheels, both front and rear, are spread farther apart to keep them as cemented to the road as the pavement itself.

There's an interior in Monza models that

reminds you of those you've seen in some frighteningly expensive sports cars. Bucket seats, door-to-door deep-twist carpeting, business-like control panel with all the dials grouped into a cockpit-like cluster.

There's a whole brand-new top-of-the-line series of Corvairs for '65 called *Corsa* with special trim, special instrumentation and very special performance. The standard rear engine is 140 hp or there's a new 180-hp Turbo-Charged version that you can add instead.

We can't help but feel that the '65 Corvair is the new sporty American car Europeans

will be clamoring to import. We can't help but feel you're going to be clamoring, too. So hurry and see one now at your Chevrolet dealer's. Then try to give up the idea of buying one. Just try. . . . Chevrolet Division of General Motors, Detroit, Michigan.

Please turn the page for more that's new.

Chevrolet's peculiar Corvair was far from an unqualified success when it debuted in 1960, partly because it used technology too far outside the automotive mainstream for the buying public's comfort. Still, in many ways, the Corvair influenced all future cars designed for and marketed to younger buyers.

plugs would load up with carbon, and the ignition didn't have enough strength to shoot spark through the carbon buildup. The cars never quite ran right on the street until they got a functional electronic ignition."

Solutions to ignition problems would come. For the time being, the simplest solution was to drive your car as if you stole it. Gas was cheap, so if low-speed running causes problems, run at high speeds. A more immediate challenge for Detroit's auto manufacturers was developing a car to sell to the baby boom generation, who had finally begun buying cars in numbers commensurate with the size of their population. The leading edge of the vast swell of children born in the years after World War II were graduating from high school and entering the work force. They had money to spend and they liked to spend it on new cars. "They weren't called 'baby boomers' yet," Jim Wangers says, "but they were coming. They were just beginning to recognize this wonderful thing called 'personal mobility.'"

This new breed of auto buyer wanted power, and the cars Detroit produced in the early 1960s did not lack power. Chevrolet's Mark II 427 racing engine generated an estimated 520 horsepower, enough to satisfy anyone. But these young consumers wanted more than just power. They wanted style. They wanted cars that turned heads when they cruised down the Main Streets of America's towns and cities. They wanted cars that did not look like their parents' cars, the cars in which Detroit manufacturers mounted their powerful V-8 engines. They wanted smaller, sportier cars. More often than not, they were young men who wanted cars that would impress the opposite sex.

Sex appeal played a key role in marketing cars to boomers. In the youth-oriented culture that was emerging in the early 1960s, the automobile became a critical component in quantifying its owner's sex appeal. This generation had a different set of standards than their parents, and chaperones were as *passé* as tail fins. To put it indelicately, the driver of a cool car was more likely to score after a Friday-night football game than the driver of a nerdy car.

This new generation, itself the result of rampant sexual activity, scored more often than did any previous generation since the fall of the Roman Empire, thanks in large part to a new technology: the birth-control pill. On May 9, 1960, the Food and Drug Administration approved the first oral contraceptive for legal use in the United States. The pill revolutionized

sexual activity. As long as human animals have roamed the earth, young people have found themselves in the eye of a hormonal hurricane. In spite of the best efforts of organized religion, this age group has always engaged in recreational sex. At best, religion has met with limited success in curbing the hormonal excess of the young. But the fear of unwanted pregnancy has historically proven more effective at keeping a lid on the sexual pressure cooker. The pill removed that inhibition and effectively blew that lid off. By the time the classic muscle car era began in 1964, American youngsters had begun to exercise their newfound sexual freedom. While society had not quite entered the era of free love, recreational sex had been heavily discounted.

In 1962 Chevrolet introduced the Chevy II, a small sedan that was as conventional as the Corvair was unconventional. Initially, the sportiest model in the Chevy II lineup was the Nova. In 1963 Chevrolet introduced an SS version of the Nova.

SMALLER, SPORTIER, SEXIER

Sex was becoming a national obsession, and smaller, sportier cars were tools that young people used to help satisfy that obsession. Detroit offered smaller, though the small autos American automakers first marketed to boomers were far from sporty. In the 1950s, American Motors Corporation had stayed afloat on the profits of its Rambler, one of the

The 1963 Nova SS—especially the convertible—was designed to be a sporty car that appealed to the growing number of younger car buyers entering the market. It had almost everything it needed to do just that.

The 1963 Chevy II Nova SS featured the same sporty accoutrements as the Monza version of the Corvair: bucket seats, extra gauges, and special trim. It also featured an engine with the same number of cylinders as the Corvair.

first compact American cars. Since the Rambler didn't offer a V-8 engine, a design that General Motors and Chrysler relied on to market their cars, AMC marketed the fuel economy of the Rambler's inline-six-cylinder engine. To boomers, the fuel-efficient Rambler was as exciting as Grandma's broken-English stories about pickling fish in the old country and as sexy as the garters holding up her support hose. The Rambler floated AMC's financial boat, but customers swayed by its practicality were more likely to be support-hose-wearing immigrants than their baby-boom grandchildren. To reach the younger generation, manufacturers needed to build cars that were smaller *and* sexy.

In typical Robert McNamara fashion, Ford grasped the "smaller" part but couldn't get its corporate head around the "sexy" part. On October 8, 1959, Ford introduced the decidedly unsexy Falcon. Basically a shrunken version of its larger sedans, the Falcon sold extremely well and earned a profit for Ford, but it failed to ignite the passion of younger buyers. Worse for Ford, McNamara had similarly small, but even uglier cars percolating through the planning processes. A few years later Lee Iacocca would reshape the Falcon

Stylized SS wheel covers comprised an important part of the SS trim package. The "6" on the quarter panel badge refers to the number of cylinders residing under the hood.

into one of the sexiest small cars on the market, creating a machine that would ignite the automotive lust of nearly every member of the baby-boom generation and in the process create an entirely new market niche: the pony car. But that was in the future; in 1960 the Falcon was simply a diminutive portion of the same-old same-old from Ford.

Ford broke little new ground with its new small car. Chevrolet not only broke new ground, it pulverized it into fine dust. The division's Corvair, introduced for the 1960 model year, used technology never before seen on an American-made automobile. Standing only 51.3 inches tall and measuring just 66.9 inches wide, the Corvair took up less garage space than any other car rolling out of Detroit at that time. The Corvair was the smallest American-made car of its day and it was easily the most peculiar. Its engine, an air-cooled opposed six-cylinder, sat in the rear of the car where it drove the rear wheels through a transaxle transmission.

The Corvair's drivetrain layout may have looked peculiar when compared to the other cars Detroit offered, but when compared to the cars being imported from Europe it seemed less so. Historically, imported cars had comprised a miniscule portion of the U.S. auto market. But as the U.S. auto industry entered the 1960s, that situation had begun to change. Imported car sales doubled between 1958 and 1959, a fact that didn't escape General Motors. The most popular import, the German-built Volkswagen, used the same technology as the Corvair: rear-mounted, air-cooled engine driving the rear wheels through a transaxle transmission. In 1960, Volkswagen sold nearly 160,000 of its peculiar little sedans.

The Corvair sold well enough in its first year to avoid being considered a dismal failure—250,000 units—but just barely. Ford sold nearly half a million Falcons in 1960, indicating that while buyers wanted a small car, they feared peculiar.

The heart of the Chevy II Nova SS package was its 194-cubic-inch inline-six-cylinder engine. Its 120 ponies were enough to give the little car more-than-adequate acceleration. But by 1963 more than adequate was not enough. The buying public was drunk on V-8 horsepower and did not get excited about Chevrolet's venerable six-cylinder.

CHEVY'S SENSIBLE SHOES

Chevrolet's designers realized that they had ventured too far outside the comfort zone of most American auto buyers with the Corvair. To cash in on the emerging market for small cars they would have to create a smaller version of the large sedans Americans were comfortable buying. That's exactly what Chevrolet introduced in September of 1961. The Chevy II was as conventional as the Corvair was peculiar. The only unconventional technology that Chevrolet used on the Chevy II was unitized-body construction. This advanced method of building cars used an integrated frame and body instead of placing a separate body on top of a ladder-type frame, the method that had been in use since the dawn of the automotive age.

The sportiest, sexiest model in the Chevy II lineup was the Nova 400, powered by a 194-cubic-inch inline six producing 120 horsepower. This was enough to give the sub-2,600-pound coupe adequate acceleration, but not enough to impress buyers lusting after 409 Impalas. The Chevy II sold better than the Corvair—Chevy dealers moved 325,000 units for 1962—but not well enough to outsell the Falcon.

To attract the growing number of young buyers, the Chevy II needed V-8 power. Even Ford understood this, and in 1963 produced a V-8-powered version of the Falcon: the Futura Sprint. Chevrolet responded with a sporty SS package for the Chevy II, which featured special trim, bucket seats, and enhanced instrumentation, but still no V-8. The Nova SS retained Chevy's unsporting inline six.

In 1964 the Chevy II finally got a proper V-8. Although not a fire-breather like the 427-cubic-inch Mark II big-block race motor, the two-barrel 283-cubic-inch small-block V-8 in the Chevy II produced 195 horsepower, enough to propel the diminutive Chevrolet through the quarter-mile traps in 18 seconds.

While the new V-8 was enough to push the Chevy II through the quarter-mile in a respectable time, it wasn't enough to push it ahead of the competition in the marketplace. Chevy II sales fell 48 percent in 1964. While this may have been due in part to a lack of power and speed, a greater factor in the slow sales of the 1964 Chevy II was the stiff competition the car faced for baby-boomer dollars. Even Chevrolet had developed a sportier car for the youth market, the Chevelle, a car that undoubtedly cannibalized quite a few Chevy II sales in Chevrolet dealerships around the country.

CHEVROLET'S TARGET MARKET CAR

After scaring customers away with the peculiar Corvair and then failing to capture a large portion of the emerging youth market with the Chevy II, Chevrolet designers wanted to avoid a third strike. The division needed to build something small, sporty, and sexy if it

wanted to secure its position as the world's number one auto manufacturer for the foreseeable future. It had to avoid a potentially risky technological revolution, as with Corvair technology, but it also needed to avoid creating a car that was too conservative, like the Chevy II. The safest path to success was to split the difference between the two: create a car that used technology the market would accept, yet one that was also sexy enough to attract young buyers.

The quickest way to get on this safest path was to build a car using an existing design. General Motors had the perfect design in its corporate parts bin with the A-body, the platform under development for Buick's Special and Oldsmobile's F-85. In physical mass, this platform fell midway between the little Chevy II and Chevrolet's full-sized models. In GM-speak this made the platform an "intermediate" car. Pontiac was using the A-body

After its spotty attempts to market the Corvair at younger buyers, and less-than-hoped-for sales of the Chevy II, Chevrolet decided to take the safest path available when introducing its new Chevelle for the 1964 model year. The new Chevelle was a thoroughly conventional car by any measure.

The Chevelle may have been conventional, but it was sleek, powerful, and sexy—just what the bourgeoning number of younger buyers wanted in a car.

The futuristic styling of the Corvair had scared away customers, so with the new Chevelle, Chevrolet's designers adhered to the lines and proportions of its larger sedans.

The 1963 Chevy II Nova SS lacked one essential ingredient to appeal to the youth market: a hot V-8. Chevrolet rectified that situation with the new Chevelle, offering a line of V-8s that included the 300-horsepower, 327-cubic-inch L74.

platform to replace its troublesome "rope-drive" Tempest and it proved the ideal design to propel Chevrolet into the consciousness of the baby boomers. The car Chevy designers created, the Chevelle, was everything the division needed: small, sporty and, most importantly, sexy.

In late August of 1963, Bunkie Knudsen, who was promoted out of Pontiac and now headed up General Motor's Chevrolet division, unveiled the new Chevelle to the automotive press to much applause. They literally applauded, according to a report in the August 30, 1963 issue of *Time* magazine. They certainly weren't applauding the car's technology—with its small-block V-8 engine and conventional body-on-frame construction, the car was basically a slightly smaller version of the Chevrolet sedans that had first carried the company's

By 1964, bucket seats and a floor-mounted shifter were prerequisites for a sporty car aimed at younger buyers.

Turbo-Fire V-8 engines in 1955. What they were applauding was the new Chevelle's style. With its sleek lines and sporty proportions, the car looked right for the market. It looked sexy.

The sexiest version of the new Chevelle, the Malibu SS, featured all the same parts as the Chevy II's new variant, the Nova SS—special trim, bucket seats, enhanced instrumentation—but it featured the critical component the 1963 Nova SS lacked: V-8 power, and quite a lot of it when all the right option boxes were checked. Initially, the hottest engine was the L77, a 220-horse 283-cubic-inch V-8 featuring a Rochester four-barrel carburetor, a 9.25:1 compression ratio, and dual exhaust. When mated to an optional Muncie M20 four-speed transmission and a 3.36:1 Posi-Traction rear differential, the Malibu SS traveled through the quarter-mile a full second quicker than its smaller Chevy II brethren. Later in the year Chevrolet offered the optional L74 V-8, a hotter 327-cubic-inch engine that generated 300 horsepower. Had the marketplace status quo from previous years remained unchanged, this L74 package might have been *the* car to buy in 1964.

The sexiest version of the new Chevelle was the Malibu SS, which featured the same special trim, bucket seats, and enhanced instrumentation as the Nova SS.

Chevrolet designers were adept at finding surfaces to adorn with SS badges. Even visually impaired passengers could quickly discern that they were riding in an SS model.

THE BARRACUDA JOINS THE FRAY

Like Ford and General Motors, Chrysler introduced a small car for the 1960 model year: the Valiant. Like the Falcon, the Valiant featured relatively conventional technology, at least compared to the Corvair, but the car's styling, from its trapezoidal grill to the spare tire shape embossed into the trunk lid, pushed into unconventional territory. The engine, another pushrod, inline six, used no cutting-edge technology, but it was oriented in a creative way. Chrysler engineers rotated this new power plant 30 degrees to the right, earning it the nickname "slant six." Designers rotated the engine to make room for a lower hood, a prerequisite for the sporty, sexy look young buyers seemed to crave. In stock form the engine produced 101 horsepower, but if a buyer installed the "Power Pak" kit they could purchase from their Chrysler dealer's parts man, the little 171-cubic-inch engine produced 148 horsepower. The Power Pak contained enough good stuff to put oak in any true hot-rodder's timber: long-runner intake manifold and bigger carburetor, high-compression pistons, and long duration camshaft.

Plymouth introduced the Barracuda in 1964, a sporty version of the Valiant economy sedan aimed at the baby boom generation.

The most obvious change in the transformation from Valiant to Barracuda was the addition of a huge glass hatchback. This provided the car with what Chrysler designers deemed a sporty profile, along with acres of storage space behind the rear seat.

Originally not branded as either a Dodge or a Plymouth, the Valiant had been sold at both dealerships. In 1961, Chrysler branded the Valiant as a Plymouth and Dodge introduced its own version, the Lancer. Chrysler's engineers tweaked their new slant six to produce 145 horsepower in stock form and 195 horses when equipped with a Power Pak. These were respectable numbers, but the engine was still a six-cylinder trying to compete in a V-8 world. Chrysler redesigned the car for 1963 and sales increased, but the lack of a V-8 engine still hampered the car's reception in the marketplace.

At the time, Chrysler's small-block engine, the A-block, had been in production since 1956, almost an eternity, given the fast pace of engine development at that time. For 1964, Chrysler engineers redesigned the A-block, creating the compact, high-revving LA series of engines. The main technological change in the transformation from A-block to LA series involved the method used to cast the engine block. Chrysler's new "thin-wall" casting technique resulted in a more-compact, lighter power plant that easily fit in the engine bay of a small car like the Valiant. Switching from the old polyspherical head design to a more-modern wedge design also helped make the new small-block engine series more contemporary. Originally displacing 273 cubic inches and producing 180 horsepower, this new small-block engine went on to become one of the most beloved power plants of the classic muscle car era, powering such iconic cars as the Challenger T/A and AAR 'Cuda, but it wasn't terribly successful when introduced.

Not that there was anything wrong with the engine, nor with the Barracuda, a sporty, fastback version of the Valiant in which Chrysler mounted the mill. Chrysler designers created the fastback look by grafting a large wrap-around rear window onto the basic Valiant. The car received a sporty interior with bucket seats clad in "glamorous gold, rich blue or black, or bright red" vinyl, according to a period sales brochure. Other than that, only a revised grille distinguished the Barracuda from a garden-variety Valiant. Budget constraints kept Chrysler's designers from deviating much further from the base car.

Perhaps the Barracuda retained a bit too much of the donor Valiant's proletarian styling for young buyers, which may have hurt its reception in the youth market, but more likely Plymouth's new sporty coupe suffered from the same problem as Chevrolet's V-8-powered Chevy II and Chevelle: stiff competition. Had the V-8-powered Barracuda been unleashed upon the American public two or three years earlier, it might have become the stuff of legends. Unfortunately for Chrysler and Chevrolet, Pontiac had beaten them to the punch.

The rear taillight housing of the Barracuda rose above the sloping hatchback to create a vestigial fin, harkening back to the massive tailfins of the 1950s.

GRAN TURISMO OMOLOGATO

Like other American automakers, Pontiac had marketed a small car in the early 1960s. A year after Chevrolet unleashed its high-tech Corvair on the American public, Pontiac introduced its Tempest. Developed jointly with Buick and Oldsmobile as part of GM's X-body program, the Tempest started life as a front-engined derivative of Chevrolet's peculiar rear-engined Corvair. The X-bodies shared the Corvair's basic unibody chassis, stretched 4 inches to attain a stature more fitting for upscale nameplates like Pontiac, Buick, or Oldsmobile. The engines would be mounted in the front instead of the rear, and the Pontiac, Buick, and Oldsmobile cars would not use Chevrolet's opposed, air-cooled, six-cylinder engines, necessitating a taller front hood. Because of this, the profiles of GM's other X-bodies would bear little resemblance to the Corvair.

Bunkie Knudsen, still heading Pontiac at that time, did not want to produce a cookie-cutter version of the small cars being introduced by sister divisions Oldsmobile and Buick, so he had his engineers develop innovative technology to distinguish his division's version of the X-body platform. Pontiac engineers created a new four-cylinder engine by splitting its 389-cubic-inch V-8 in half. Displacing 195 cubic inches, huge for a four-cylinder, the engine produced ample horsepower and torque; unfortunately, it also produced excessive vibration. Modern large-displacement four-cylinder engines can resort to technology like balance shafts to quell engine vibration, but such technology wasn't available to Pontiac designers at that time. Instead, they resorted to an innovative system nicknamed the "rope-drive" because it used a flexible drive-shaft woven from strands of high-tensile steel like a rope. This flexible driveshaft, which connected the rear engine housing to a transaxle transmission between the rear wheels, absorbed the engine's thunderous vibration remarkably well, keeping it from intruding on the passenger compartment.

The vinyl covering the seats in this 1964 Barracuda was "glamorous gold," according to a period advertising brochure.

With the high-tech Tempest, the reach of Pontiac's engineers exceeded their technological grasp. Even though the passengers were isolated from the vibration, it was still there, pounding the duck butter out of the engine and drivetrain. Engine vibration hammered the nylon timing gears back into raw petroleum. Worse yet, the rear-mounted transaxle wasn't strong enough to handle the power put out by the oversized four-banger engine. Fragile transmissions and timing-gear wear caused by the engine vibration doomed the high-tech Pontiac in the marketplace.

For 1964, Pontiac planned to replace the Tempest with a car based on GM's upcoming A-body platform. With this car, Pontiac's marketing team faced a two-fold challenge. Not only did they need to overcome the negative publicity generated by the failure of the rope-drive Tempest; they also needed to discover an entirely new method for reaching the youth market, since the tool the division had relied on since the 1950s—racing—was no longer an option.

General Motors' total ban on racing involvement hurt Pontiac more than any other GM division. Pontiac's advertising had been built around racing success, and that advertising was finally starting to pay off when GM announced the racing ban for 1963.

Automobile enthusiasts were just beginning to view Pontiac as GM's performance division. The corporate racing ban seemed like a death sentence for Pontiac, but Jim Wangers saw it as an opportunity.

"Pontiac had carefully planned the image of its new cars," Wangers says. "They were quick on the street, but we knew that racing performance wasn't the only way to sell these cars. When that stage (racing) was abolished, we needed to keep our cars in the performance limelight." In his book *Glory Days*, Wangers describes how Pontiac's Chief

In addition to copious cargo capacity, the Barracuda provided class-leading handling, thanks to its advanced torsion bar front suspension design, and the car proved successful in SCCA racing.

Plymouth adorned its new Barracuda with badges featuring the car's namesake fish.

Engineer John DeLorean and his two favorite staff engineers, Bill Collins and Russ Gee, came up with an inspired way to keep Pontiac cars in the performance limelight:

> Delorean planned regular "What If?" sessions at the GM proving grounds in Milford, Michigan, on Saturday mornings. . . . It was very early spring, 1963. A prototype 1964 Tempest Coupe equipped with a 326-cubic-inch engine was on a lift. DeLorean, Collins, and Gee were under the car, discussing the chassis. Collins casually mentioned, "You know, John, with the engine mounts being the same [a result of Pontiac's early decision to develop one family of engines rather than a big-block family and a small-block family], it would take us about 20 minutes to slip a 389 into this thing. We'll probably need some heavier springs in the front end, but the engine will fit right in."
>
> John looked at him, caught an approving nod from Gee, and without uttering another word they were all in agreement.
>
> One week later the group at the Saturday morning session was greeted by a prototype 1964 Tempest coupe with a 389 engine in it.

Though unusual looking thanks to its bulging rear window, Plymouth's new car for the youth market was handsome enough and might have been more popular had it not been introduced in the same model year as the Chevelle, GTO, and Mustang.

That Saturday morning in Michigan marked the moment the muscle car era kicked off. It took one drive in the prototype DeLorean, Collins, and Gee had created to realize that this was the car that would meet the needs of the new baby-boom market: a sporty, intermediate-sized car with big V-8 power. DeLorean named the car GTO, an acronym of the Italian *Gran Turismo Omologato*, "Grand Touring Homologated."

Conceiving, naming, and developing the GTO proved to be the easy part. The hard part was getting the car approved by the fun police at General Motors, who were more concerned with staying under the Justice Department's radar than creating the perfect car for the baby-boom generation. In addition to banning corporate involvement in racing, the fun police had instituted a policy limiting GM cars to 10 pounds per cubic inch. According to that formula, the largest power plant DeLorean could mount in his 3,500-pound GTO's engine bay would displace 350 cubic inches.

Cargo space was one of the Barracuda's selling points, and that space could be expanded dramatically by lowering the rear seatback.

Unlike its donor car, the Valiant, the new Barracuda featured the main ingredient needed for a car to succeed in the baby boom market: a V-8 engine. In its original form, this small-block V-8 displaced 273 cubic inches and produced 180 horsepower.

In 1963, Pontiac's Chief Engineer John DeLorean and his two favorite staff engineers, Bill Collins and Russ Gee, bolted a 389-cubic-inch engine in Pontiac's upcoming Tempest intermediate sedan. The resulting car, the GTO, forever changed the automotive landscape.

Pete Estes, by that time Pontiac's division manager, and his band of mavericks needed to find a creative loophole to save General Motors' corporate pinheads from themselves. They learned that the committee that oversaw such minutia as displacement-to-weight ratios only scrutinized new models and didn't inspect option packages, so Pontiac made the GTO an option package for the two-door LeMans, which was to be Pontiac's counterpart to Chevrolet's Malibu. To further ensure that the GTO would pass GM's corporate muster, Estes and DeLorean presold 5,000 units before GM management found out about the car's existence. This made it all but impossible for GM management to kill the GTO without looking like the world's biggest collection of incompetents in front of its dealer network. It's easier to ask forgiveness than permission, "especially," as Wangers notes, "when you sell every one you make."

Pontiac rolled out the GTO in late 1963 with minimal fanfare. Pete Estes' outlaw division had slipped the car past GM's corporate fun police, but just barely. They wanted to avoid poking an angered GM management with a stick and further angering them. The corporation had let the rogues at Pontiac have their way, and they were happy to sell an additional 5,000 LeMans coupes, but they made it clear that this would be a one-time exemption. "'We don't want to see any more,'" Wangers quotes corporate brass in *Glory Days*. "'Remember, just 5,000.'" Pontiac limited initial advertising to black-and-white inserts in enthusiast magazines.

While sexy enough to appeal to the newly important youth market, the revolutionary nature of the car wasn't immediately obvious. A casual glance at a 1964 GTO revealed a car that looked like an upscale version of Chevrolet's sporty Malibu. Popping open the

With the 1964 GTO, Pontiac created the car the automotive world had been screaming for—a light, sporty, sexy hot rod with big V-8 power.

The huge number of younger customers swelling the ranks of the car-buying public in late 1963 approved of the new GTO and the car was an unqualified success. Though General Motors had originally told Pontiac it could produce no more than 5,000 GTOs, Pontiac sold more than 32,000 units by the end of the 1964 model year.

When equipped with Pontiac's Tri-Power option—a trio of Rochester two-barrel carburetors—the 389-cubic-inch engine in the 1964 GTO produced 348 horsepower.

hood, however, made it clear to even the most obtuse observer that the revolution had indeed begun. Generating 325 horsepower, the standard 389-cubic-inch GTO engine was the most massive V-8 yet seen in a car of its size. A Carter four-barrel carburetor pumped its fuel charge through a dual-plane intake manifold into heads pilfered from the division's mighty 421-cubic-inch HO engine. That fuel charge needed to be of the high-octane variety to placate the 10.75:1 compression ratio without inducing detonation. Specially hardened cast Arma-Steel rods connected the flat-top aluminum pistons to the cast pearlitic malleable iron crankshaft. Serious speed freaks ordered the optional M21 close-ratio four-speed transmission connected to a stout 3.90:1 gear set residing in the 10-bolt rear differential housing. Stump-pulling ratios of 4.11:1 and 4.33:1 were available as dealer-installed options. By December 1963, Pontiac had made available the Tri-Power engine option, which added a trio of Rochester two-barrel carburetors and bumped power output to 348 ponies.

With this setup, the performance of the GTO was so strong that fans invented a new nickname for the GTO: "the GreaT One." Everything worked perfectly, with the exception of the tires, especially on cars equipped with the M21 transmission option. They were just too skinny to handle all the torque the drivetrain produced. "You could launch the GTO from a standing start and burn rubber to infinity," Wangers writes in *Glory Days*.

Because of the almost complete lack of publicity, initial sales didn't look as though they would break through the 5,000-unit limit GM management had specified, but the GTO was simply too good a car to remain inconspicuous. Word-of-mouth publicity proved to be enough to generate strong sales for a car that so perfectly captured the qualities the baby-boom market desired, at a price they could live with. With a base price of $2,776, almost anyone could afford a new GTO. By the time 1964 rolled around, sales had begun to pick up.

A test that appeared in the March 1964 issue of *Car and Driver* magazine pitted a Pontiac GTO against a Ferrari GTO, one of the most exclusive and exotic automobiles in the world. The cars didn't actually compete head to head, except in an oil painting commissioned for the magazine's cover, and performance numbers weren't exactly fair, since Jim Wangers now admits he secretly replaced the test car's stock 389-cubic-inch engine with a tweaked 421-cubic-inch HO motor. Wangers, who attended the test, also knew the flawed quarter-mile testing procedure the magazine used was producing numbers bordering on fantasy, but he had no interest in correcting them. Quarter-mile

times of 13.1 seconds in the spec box and photos of Pontiac's baby-boom car sitting on the test track next to a mighty Ferrari gave the Pontiac instant credibility. Recognizing that this story compared apples to oranges, the writer asked if, in Pontiac's case, the GTO initials hadn't stood for "Going Too far Overboard?" No matter. GTO sales exploded upon publication of the article.

GTO sales for the 1964 model year totaled 32,450 units. This was on top of sales of the base Tempest and LeMans models, and thus represented an unbudgeted financial windfall for General Motors. While a car like the GTO infuriated GM's fun police, ultimately General Motors was a corporation, and the goal of any corporation is to earn a profit. The GTO option most certainly earned a profit for the Pontiac division.

Though they stood for "Gran Turismo Omologato," or "Grand Touring Homologated" when translated from Italian to English, the letters "GTO" quickly earned Pontiac's new muscle car the nickname "The GreaT One."

OLDSMOBILE AWAKENS

The success of Pontiac's GTO lit a fire under other U.S. auto manufacturers. Suddenly everyone wanted to jump into the muscle car game and get as many baby-boom dollars as possible. The GTO might have been a cash cow for Pontiac, but it also became a target at which every other automaker in the United States was about to take aim. In particular, Pontiac's sister divisions Oldsmobile, Buick, and Chevrolet chafed at being outsmarted by Pontiac. These divisions had a distinct advantage over Ford and Chrysler—they had their own A-body cars that were, for all practical purposes, versions of the GTO. However, GM's other divisions' earlier decisions to pursue separate small-block and big-block engine families meant that dropping larger engines in the bays of their A-body cars would take a lot longer than the 20 minutes it took Bill Collins and Russ Gee to create the first GTO.

Oldsmobile wasted little time creating a GTO competitor. The division had little time to waste. It needed all the help it could get when trying to develop a car for the youth market. The company that had earned a reputation as General Motors' performance division when it introduced the Rocket 88 V-8 in 1949 had become GM's aging spinster by 1964, selling stodgy conservative sedans that held little appeal for the baby boomers. Olds had attempted to gain a foothold in the emerging youth market with its F-85 version of the GM X-body platform, but that attempt was less than successful. Even though the F-85 had the prerequisite V-8 engine from the very beginning—the aluminum-block "Rockette"—the F-85 was one of the industry's slowest-

Pontiac equipped the GTO with an elegant, luxurious interior, complete with a turned-metal dash filled with a host of esoteric gauges and switches.

selling small cars. Even the lowly Studebaker Lark outsold Oldsmobile's smallest model.

With the GTO, Pontiac had shown Oldsmobile the path to performance redemption. In the middle of the 1964 model year, Oldsmobile introduced a muscle car option package for its F-85 Cutlass with big V-8 power, or at least as big as Oldsmobile could offer without extensively redesigning its version of the A-body chassis. Dubbed the 4-4-2 (which stood for four-speed, four-barrel, dual-exhaust), Oldsmobile initially gave its car a souped-up version of the division's 330-cubic-inch V-8 engine. While this engine produced 290 horsepower, putting it on par with the 300-horsepower Chevy Malibu SS, neither version of GM's A-body could compete with the 348-horsepower Tri-Power GTO. More importantly, neither car could touch the massive 428 ft-lb of torque the bigger Pontiac engine produced.

For the 1965 model year, General Motors' accountants, having tallied the contribution the GTO had made to the corporate bottom line, twisted the arms of GM's corporate fun police and made them relent on their 10-pounds-per-cubic-inch rule. GM raised the displacement limit of its intermediate cars to 400 cubic inches. This allowed the good corporate soldiers at Oldsmobile to stuff a proper big-block engine in the bay of the 4-4-2, a version of the 425-cubic-inch engine Oldsmobile used in its larger sedans with the bore reduced just enough to skirt under the new corporate displacement limit. With the bigger engine in place, the 4-4-2 (the initial "4" now standing for "400 cubic inches," since Oldsmobile offered an optional automatic transmission in addition to a four-speed-manual for the 1965 model year) produced 345 horsepower, making it a match for Pontiac's great one.

The GTOs skinny tires proved to be the weak link when transmitting the Tri-Power 389s torque to the pavement.

Oldsmobile was the first to respond to Pontiac's GTO with its 4-4-2, introduced as a mid-year 1964 model. The 4-4-2 stood for 4-speed, 4-barrel, dual-exhaust, and was *not* related to engine displacement, which was 330 cubic inches. For 1965, Oldsmobile shoehorned a proper big-block V-8 into the engine bay.

Initially Chevrolet responded to the GTO by putting increasingly more powerful small-block V-8 engines in its Chevelle intermediate car, but by 1965, it was clear that big-block power was needed. The Malibu SS 396, internally coded the Z-16, featured a 396-cubic-inch street-going version of Chevrolet's Mark II NASCAR racing engine.

CHEVROLET PUMPS UP ITS CHEVELLE

Like Oldsmobile, Chevrolet initially followed the corporate displacement regulations and opted for a stronger small-block engine to compete with the big-cube GTO. In 1964 Chevrolet built approximately 12 Chevelles with 365-horsepower 327-cubic-inch Corvette engines. Dealers sold these cars for $900 over their sticker price, indicating a strong demand for high-powered Chevelles. In 1965 Chevrolet borrowed the 350-horsepower 327-cubic-inch V-8—one of the strongest small-blocks in its stable—from the Corvette. Regular Production Option (RPO) L79 (as the engine was known internally) used a Holley four-barrel carburetor, big-valve heads, 11.0:1 compression, and, surprisingly, hydraulic lifters to produce a whopping 360 ft-lb of torque. When the power was transmitted through a 3.70:1 rear end, the tires proved the limiting factor in getting good quarter-mile times.

The 6,021 Chevelles equipped with RPO L79 ub 1965 made great street racers, but Pontiac's GTO had created the archetype for the muscle car: a big engine in a midsized car. Once the buying public developed a craving for such a beast, nothing less would satisfy that craving. To compete, Chevrolet needed a bigger power plant, something Chevy designers had been toying with for some time. As early as 1963, Vince Piggins, who headed up the development of Chevrolet's performance products, had begun working on a Chevelle with a version of the Mark II racing engine that had effectively been killed when GM banned corporate involvement in racing. When GM raised the displacement limit for the A-body cars to 400 cubic inches, Piggins' team had its design ready, and in February 1965, Chevrolet unveiled a version of the Chevelle that was a true muscle car.

Chevrolet produced the Malibu SS 396 on an extremely limited basis, building just 201 for the 1965 model year. The following year would see Chevelles equipped with big-block engines go into mass production.

By 1965 Buick had also entered the muscle car market with its Gran Sport. Like Pontiac, Buick started with its version of the intermediate A-body chassis, the Skylark, and stuffed a big V-8 engine in it.

The car, the Malibu SS 396, equipped with what Chevrolet coded the Z16 package, contained everything needed to make baby boomers salivate. Designed as a luxury-performance car, the Z16 Malibu featured every creature comfort on Chevrolet's option list: clock, tachometer, 160-miles-per-hour speedometer, four-speaker AM/FM stereo. But the feature that really triggered the Pavlovian responses of younger buyers lurked under the hood: a street-going version of the infamous big-block Mark II mystery motor. The 396-cubic-inch engine, which pumped out a class-leading 375 horsepower, retained all the best high-performance bits of the race-only engine, right down to the high-tech "porcupine" heads, so named because of the staggered arrangement of the valves.

Unfortunately, the Z16 version of the Malibu SS 396 was expensive—the price topped $4,100—and exclusive. Chevrolet built just 201 examples, making the model one of the rarest muscle cars of the era. Volume production of Chevelles equipped with 396-cubic-inch big-block engines would not commence until a restyled version of the car debuted for the 1966 model year.

WHEN A BETTER MUSCLE CAR IS BUILT, BUICK WILL BUILD IT

In 1964, Pontiac owned its title as GM's performance division, having wrestled it from Oldsmobile. But prior to Oldsmobile's usurping of that title on the strength of the division's Rocket 88 OHV V-8, Buick had held it for decades. Buick's Fireball Eight, an inline eight-cylinder—a design known as the "straight eight"—had powered performance cars like the Century since the 1930s. Throughout the intervening years, Buick had always kept sporty performance cars in its lineup and the division jumped at the opportunity to battle Pontiac in the intracorporate muscle car wars that raged within General Motors after the introduction of the GTO.

When GM relaxed the ban on larger displacement engines in the corporate A-body chassis for 1965, Buick followed the lead of Chevrolet and Oldsmobile and mounted a 401-cubic-inch engine in its Gran Sport, which was a GTO-like option package for the

Since the Buick Gran Sport's dash didn't lend itself to a circular tach, Buick designers mounted it in the floor counsel in front of the shift lever.

The Gran Sport was Buick's first attempt to reach younger buyers. In 1963 Buick was already worried about the aging demographics of its customer base.

division's A-body car, the Skylark. Although the engine's 325 horsepower put it at the bottom rung of the A-body performance ladder, the engine made up for its relative lack of peak power with a prodigious torque output of 445 ft-lb. This made the Gran Sport a real tire shredder when taking off from a stoplight. Smokey burn-outs impressed the neighborhood kids a lot more than did esoteric dyno charts. Besides, if an owner wanted to do some serious drag racing with his Gran Sport, he could purchase a dual carburetor manifold and a pair of four-barrel carbs from his Buick parts man.

CHRYSLER EXERCISES THE NUCLEAR OPTION

General Motors' other divisions weren't the only competition faced by the GTO. Chrysler also saw an opportunity to fatten its corporate coffers by marketing extreme performance to the budding baby-boom generation. Extreme performance was something Chrysler Corporation had in abundance. In addition to the small-block and big-block wedge engines, it had the all-conquering Hemi.

Chrysler's decision to build a production street car with the 426 Hemi came about as a result of NASCAR's rules. For the Hemi to be eligible to run on NASCAR's superspeedways, it would have to grace the engine bay of at least 500 of road-going cars to be sold to the general public. Hemi-powered cars had dominated NASCAR racing in 1964. In all, Hemi-powered Plymouths won 12 Grand National races that year and Hemi-powered Dodges won 14. The Hemi so overwhelmed the competition that the situation bordered on ludicrous. To keep the Grand National series from turning into the Chrysler Cup races, NASCAR banned the Hemi from competition for 1965 on the grounds that it was not a regular production engine.

And it was not. Chrysler had equipped a handful of pedestrian Plymouths and Dodge street cars with Hemi engines in 1964, the exact number of which is unknown,

The 1966 Hurst GeeTO Tiger was a contest car. To win the car, contestants had to correctly count how many times the word "Tiger" was mentioned in the "GeeTO Tiger" song, and explain in 25 words or less why they deserved to win.

The GeeTo Tiger featured Hurst gold paint, gold-plated Hurst wheels, and a Hurst shifter, along with a Royal Pontiac Bobcat package and a host of factory performance and luxury options.

The GeeTO Tiger may have looked a bit dandified with its gold-plated wheels and shifter, but it still had the brawn that made any GTO one of the most muscular cars of the era.

but the number was so low that few people at the time ever saw one outside of the confines of a drag strip. And calling them "street cars" was a stretch. The cars were not created on a factory assembly line, but rather were shipped to Automotive Conversions, a company that manufactured ambulances and limousines, where they were converted to stock-looking drag racing cars. The only visual clues as to what madness lurked beneath the hoods of these cars were shovel-shaped hood scoops that funneled huge amounts of fresh air to the hungry pair of four-barrel carburetors feeding the engines.

The GeeTO Tiger was as shiny underneath the hood as it was on the outside.

Dodge's first attempt to design a car specifically for the baby boom market was the Charger, a fastback version of Chrysler's new-for-1966 B-body chassis.

INSET: While the styling of the Charger might have been controversial, it offered something no other manufacturer could match: an optional Hemi engine.

While the number of these radical cars that found their way to the street is so low as to be almost negative, a few resourceful enthusiasts figured out how to acquire these mythical beasts. Lynn Ferguson, a casual drag racer from St. John, Michigan, was one such enthusiast. Tired of losing in his 1951 Ford six-cylinder, Ferguson saved up and ordered a car he knew would win races: a Super Stock Dodge 440 with a 426-cubic-inch Max Wedge in Stage III trim. After four months of waiting, he learned that Chrysler had ceased production of Max Wedge engines, but they would be replaced by another engine. Six weeks later he plunked down $3,820.25 cash and found himself the proud owner of one of the rarest American performance cars ever built. Other than the upside down shovel on the hood, one of the few clues as to the car's true nature was a sticker inside the glove compartment that read, "Notice. This car is equipped with a 426 cu. in. engine (and other special equipment). This car is intended for use in supervised acceleration trials and is not for highway or general passenger car use."

Chrysler manufactured more Hemi-powered "street cars" in 1965, but these were even further removed from the cars the company manufactured for actual street use. By this time the F/X class had superseded the Super Stock class as the premiere drag racing class (the F/X class would eventually morph into the funny car classes). The Hemi-powered cars Chrysler built in 1965 featured the altered wheelbases and lightweight materials

The Charger was designed to appeal to younger buyers, but unlike the muscle cars offered by other manufacturers it was an upscale car, loaded with features and expensive, compared to the competition.

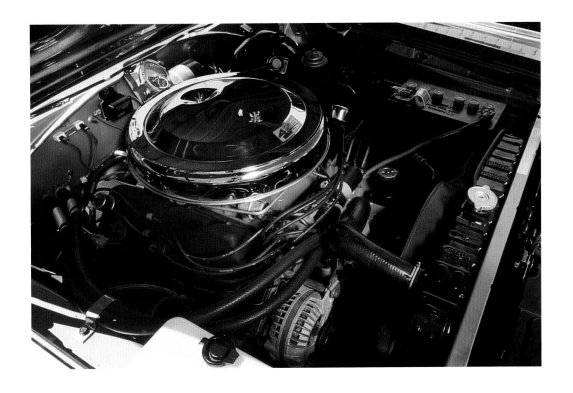

The 1966 street Hemi engine hadn't been redesigned for street use; it had simply been detuned from the racing versions. As such, it made a less-than-ideal powerplant for passenger car use, but if you wanted the ultimate performance engine, there was no other choice.

Like the earlier Barracuda, the Charger offered class-leading cargo capacity when the rear seatbacks were folded down. If you wanted to haul a lot of stuff and get it to where it needed to go quickly, you would be hard-pressed to do better than a Hemi Charger.

Though the Charger sold well enough for Chrysler in 1966, its styling just wasn't right for the market and sales fell dramatically in 1967.

INSET: The fastback roofline gave the Charger a dramatically different profile than its B-body brethren, even though much of the rest of the sheet metal was similar to other B-body models.

allowed in the F/X class. More of these cars found their way to private enthusiasts, but Hemi sightings on the street were still extremely rare, and every Hemi Chrysler built was intended as a tool for racing. Chrysler had yet to follow Pontiac's lead and design a muscle car specifically for marketing to baby boomers.

Hemis were about to become less rare. NASCAR's banishment of the Hemi from its superspeedways so angered Chrysler that it pulled all factory NASCAR-racing support for the 1965 season. In its attempt to avoid turning the Grand National series into the Chrysler Cup, NASCAR had inadvertently turned it into the Ford Cup, since Ford was the only factory still actively competing in the series. But Chrysler still wanted to race in the Grand National series, and the only way that would happen would be for the company to offer a version of its insane Hemi race engine in its passenger cars on a wider basis.

By late 1965, Hemi-powered Mopars finally roamed free on American streets; the Hemi had become a regular production option on Chrysler's new B-body cars for the 1966 model year. One new B-body model in particular was aimed squarely at the emerging muscle car market: the Dodge Charger. While the other B-body cars featured styling that wouldn't scare anyone's grandmother, the Charger had the sleek, sexy look a car needed

to go up against the likes of the GTO and Malibu SS, thanks to its sculpted fastback roofline. The Charger had other styling touches that set it apart from the crowd besides the roofline, like headlights hidden behind doors in the grille and bucket seats not only in the front, but in the back as well. The same budget constraints that kept much of the Valiant's sheet metal on the 1964 Barracuda also kept much of the Coronet's sheet metal on the Charger, but no one would confuse the two. Visually the Charger had enough unique content to distinguish it from Grandma's grocery-getter.

The Charger was a true muscle car, a sporty intermediate-sized car with big V-8 power. Pedestrian Chargers featured V-8s ranging up to a 383-cubic-inch version of the big-block wedge. If a buyer was rich enough and brave enough to spend the extra $1,105 needed to check the "Hemi" box on the option sheet, the Charger had the biggest V-8 power available. Given that Chrysler engineers only made minor changes in the transition from race

When equipped with the optional Hemi, the Charger was one of the few muscle cars that could crowd the big numbers on the usually-optimistic speedometers.

Chrysler gave the new Charger headlights that hid behind servo-operated doors in the grill. This was extremely cool when everything worked, but doors that stuck open or closed proved to be problematic as the cars aged.

engine to street engine, the street Hemi's horsepower rating, which remained the same as the race engine at 425 ponies, was still a conservative estimate by any measure. The 1966 street Hemi so closely mirrored the specifications of the earlier racing versions that Chrysler used the street version in the 110 cars it built for Super Stock drag racing in 1967, testifying to the performance potential of the design.

While the Charger sold well for Dodge, the vast majority of buyers opted for one of the wedge engines rather than the almighty Hemi. For most people the Hemi was simply too much engine. Even those people who could afford the steep asking price seldom had the skill to handle what was without question the single most powerful regular production engine of the muscle car era. The few people who did check the Hemi box on the option sheet ended up with one of the biggest, baddest power plants ever offered for public consumption. Any discussion about who had the fastest car in town ended the instant someone said, "I've got a Hemi . . . " The street Hemi might not have been the most popular choice for Charger power, but its very existence escalated the muscle car performance war to a level no one could have imagined when Pontiac bolted together the first GTO.

Although a Hemi-equipped Charger was easily the fastest car on any road it occupied, few buyers opted for the expensive Hemi option, instead settling for the standard pedestrian 383 B-block.

THE FOG OF WAR

The year 1964 saw the birth of the muscle car, a vehicle that was more of a recombination of existing parts designed for and marketed to the largest, most affluent generation in American history than it was a technological innovation. While it may have been more of a marketing triumph than an engineering triumph, without a doubt the GTO changed automotive history. It also touched off a performance war the likes of which the U.S. auto market had never seen before and has not seen since.

That year also saw an escalation of U.S. involvement in Southeast Asia. On August 2, North Vietnamese patrol boats attacked the American destroyer USS *Maddox* in the Gulf of Tonkin, 10 miles off the coast of North Vietnam. They fired three torpedoes, but only a single machine-gun round actually struck the *Maddox,* resulting in no causalities. This began a series of events that ultimately led to Secretary of Defense Robert McNamara lobbying congress to give President Johnson a free hand in dealing with the Vietnamese situation. The resulting Gulf of Tonkin Resolution gave Johnson unprecedented powers to wage war in Vietnam. During his 1964 reelection campaign Johnson vowed not to get the U.S. military involved in a war 10,000 miles away from the U.S. mainland. But even before the election, he and his advisors planned an escalation of U.S. involvement in Vietnam. By the end of the year, 23,000 U.S. "military advisors" fought alongside the South Vietnamese against the North Vietnamese Army and the Viet Cong guerrilla fighters.

Most Americans were more concerned with the horsepower ratings of the new crop of muscle cars than they were with political turmoil in a part of the world many of them had never even heard of. Few people imagined that tens of thousands of American youths would die in that part of the world by the end of the decade, decimating the generation of people for which the muscle cars had been designed. Fewer still could have foreseen that the political backlash against this war would stack the federal government with people as opposed to high-performance cars as they were to the Vietnam War.

For the time being, American auto enthusiasts enjoyed the bumper crop of high-performance muscle cars resulting from the performance war between Chrysler and the various divisions of General Motors. Chrysler in particular had escalated the conflict with the introduction of its street Hemi, the muscle car equivalent of a tactical nuclear weapon.

Ford produced some cars with respectable performance during this period, but most of them were homologation specials built in ultralow volumes to qualify cars and engines for racing programs. In the muscle car war raging in Detroit, Ford appeared to be neutral, an automotive Switzerland watching the battles from the sidelines.

But Ford wasn't absent from the performance war. They might not have been competing in the battle between the classic muscle cars—intermediate-sized cars powered by big-cubic-inch engines—but they were competing in different battles. Ford let other manufacturers define the muscle car in part because the company's designers were busy creating an entirely new breed of performance car: the pony car. ▪

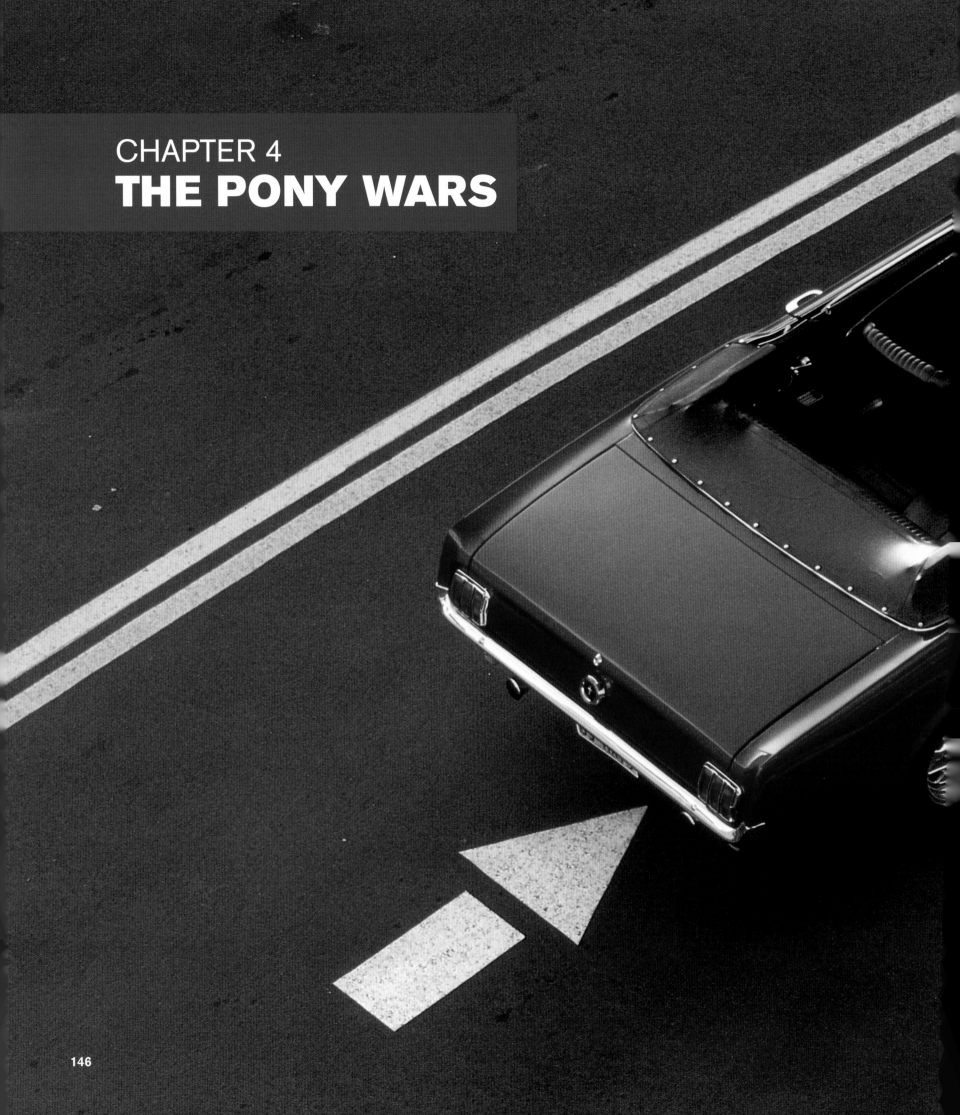

Ford's Mustang broke no new technical ground when it debuted in April 1964, but it revolutionized automotive style.

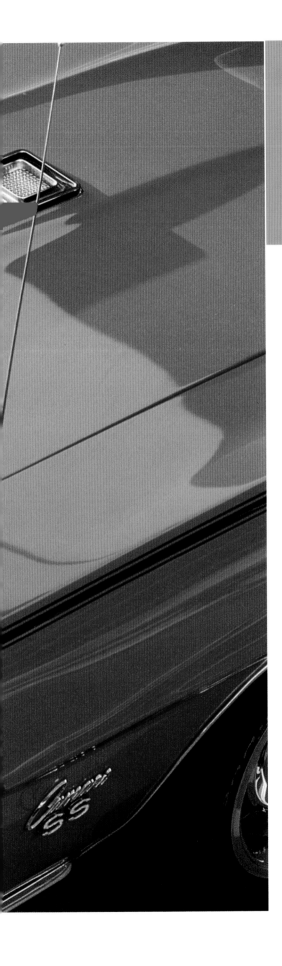

It took Chevrolet management some time to realize that the Corvair could not compete with the Mustang. The company didn't produce a legitimate challenger until the 1967 Camaro. The model shown here is a 1969 SS 350.

"**D**id we sit out the muscle car era? Well, in a sense we did," Ford's former product planning manager Don Frey says today. While it's true that Ford never really pursued the classic muscle car formula as dictated by Pontiac's GTO—big V-8 engine in an intermediate-sized coupe—that doesn't mean Ford Motor ignored the needs and desires of the emerging baby-boom market.

A casual observer might have thought the company was asleep at the wheel, but people inside Ford clearly understood what this huge new market wanted.

Lido "Lee" Iacocca was one such person. Iacocca had pondered the sales potential of an attractively styled Falcon since the car's introduction, but questioning anything about the Falcon was not a popular stance to take within the company. The two most influential people at Ford—Henry Ford II, or "the Deuce," as he was known, and Robert McNamara—had micromanaged the styling of the Falcon. First-year Falcon sales of 417,174 cars, a record number of units, indicated that their vision had been spot on for

Ford offered the new Mustang with an optional fastback roof. Baby boomers found Ford's interpretation of the fastback concept much more to their liking than they found the Plymouth Barracuda's fastback roof.

the market. It would have remained the right car for the market, had the market not changed around the car.

But, as always happens, the market did change. Chevrolet took its Corvair in a more sporting direction in its sophomore year, creating the Corvair Monza, which featured bucket seats and a four-speed transmission as standard equipment. Falcon sales rose during the car's second year on the market, but not at the rate Corvair sales rose. Falcons still outsold Corvairs nearly two-to-one, but the peculiar little Chevy had closed the gap at a rapid pace in just one year.

By that time McNamara had left for Washington, D.C.; Iacocca had been promoted to vice president and general manager of Ford Division and was now in a position to pursue his idea of a better-looking Falcon.

Iacocca not only questioned the direction his predecessor had taken with Falcon styling; he questioned the direction in which McNamara had taken the entire company. McNamara's pursuit of utilitarian transportation had been so single-minded and dogged that some within the company secretly wondered if he yearned for the days of cars painted only in black. Iacocca formed what became known as the Fairlane Committee, a team assigned to brainstorm ideas for Ford's future direction, a team that included Don Frey. One of the issues concerning the committee was the increasing share of the small car market Chevrolet's Corvair was eating up since the introduction of the Monza.

"'We started watching registrations of the Corvair, which was a dog,'" Frey told Mike Mueller in his book *Mustang 1964-1/2—1973*. "'I guess in desperation they put bucket seats in the thing, called it a Monza, and it started to sell. We got the idea that there must be something to it. And that's how it all started, watching Monzas.'"

The committee agreed that Ford needed to develop a sporty car to help shed the stodgy image McNamara had cultivated, coining the phrase "The Lively Ones" to encompass the company's new performance-oriented philosophy. In February of 1962, the committee's

The sportiest version of Ford's original Mustang was the fastback GT equipped with a K-code engine. This 289-cubic-inch small-block V-8 produced 271 horsepower.

The fastback version of the Mustang might have had the raciest lines, but the convertible, like this GT, was the car to have in 1965.

philosophy first took the form of a car made available to the public: the Falcon Futura. Like the Corvair, the Futura featured bucket seats and a four-speed transmission, prerequisites for a sporty car. Unfortunately the public was developing another prerequisite for a sporty car: a V-8 engine. The Futura featured a tarted up 170-cubic-inch inline six that generated 101 horsepower, quite a few more than the standard 144-cubic-inch engine, but it was still a six. The following year, Ford unveiled the Sprint version of the Falcon Futura. The Sprint featured Ford's newly developed small-block 260-cubic-inch V-8 that used advanced thin-wall casting techniques, resulting in a lightweight power plant perfectly suited for installation in a compact car like the Falcon.

TOTAL PERFORMANCE

The Futura Sprint proved to be one of the pivotal cars of the era, not because it was the most exciting vehicle on the market—it was far from that—but because it represented a dramatic change in Ford's corporate philosophy. A philosophy of conservatism had been championed not only by Robert McNamara, but also by Ford's young chairman, Henry Ford II. The Deuce directed his company's resources toward promoting an image of safety rather than performance.

But by 1962 even the chairman realized his philosophy needed changing. Chevrolet and Pontiac dominated NASCAR's superspeedways and Chrysler's new Max Wedge

In 1964 Ford built 190 replicas of the Mustang used to pace that year's Indianapolis 500. These are among the rarest of all Mustangs.

controlled NHRA drag strips. Ford had become practically invisible to the car-crazy baby boomers. Lee Iacocca convinced Ford that he needed to act decisively or risk losing the emerging youth market to the competition. The Deuce contacted his counterparts at General Motors and complained about the blatant violations of the AMA racing ban that were taking place at GM's Pontiac and Chevrolet divisions. The top GM brass responded that the violations had been the result of actions by rogue division managers and corporate headquarters had no way of reining in these outlaws. Ford responded with a letter stating that Ford Motor would no longer be part of the voluntary ban on factory involvement in motor sports.

By this time the Fairlane Committee's "Lively Ones" concept had evolved into "Total Performance," and the Deuce's letter, which effectively told the AMA to stuff its ban, meant that the committee could pursue total performance at the highest levels of motor racing. The team wasted no time planning Ford's return to NASCAR stock car racing and NHRA drag racing, but they didn't stop there. They also planned to build an engine to run in the prestigious Indianapolis 500. "We went after the big-ticket items in those days," Don Frey says. "How can you beat the publicity of Colin Chapman winning the Indy 500?"

The committee also began working on a car that would bring the concept of total performance to the masses. The V-8-powered Falcon Futura Sprint represented the first tentative efforts to make such a car a reality, but the committee had a much more exciting car in the wings. Lee Iacocca wanted his Ford division to produce a consumer car that truly embodied the concept of total performance and encouraged his designers to develop a sporty four-seat car. The assignment eventually fell to Frey and his assistant Hal Sperlich.

This 1965 convertible features the hot K-code engine, which made the lightweight Mustang a match for full-blown muscle cars, like Pontiac's GTO, in a stoplight drag race.

Frey and Sperlich were charged with creating a "special Falcon," a sporty 2+2-seat car (a car with minimal rear seats) based on the Falcon chassis. The car was to cost no more than $2,500 and weigh no more than 2,500 pounds.

The Deuce did not share Iacocca's enthusiasm for such a car. The Falcon Futura Sprint had not sold in huge numbers and he saw no reason why the project Frey was working on would fare any better. This meant that Frey did not receive a lot of support from Ford's top brass. Where the Deuce went, so did most of the rest of corporate management.

"'Nobody wanted the car,'" Frey recalls. "'The car came before the executive committee five times, and each time it got shot down. Everyone was afraid of the Edsel.'"

The Edsel debacle still loomed large in everyone's consciousness at Ford in the early 1960s. An utter marketing and sales failure, the disastrous Edsel line of cars had drained Ford Motor coffers of more than $350 million in the two short years the car had been on the market. The company was only starting to recover from the fiasco by the time Frey tried to sell his new car to the executive committee.

"Each time I proposed it," Frey continues, referring to his new sporty car design, "Mr. Ford said no. Then, finally, the afternoon after the fifth meeting, we were in the design studio looking at some new proposals. Mr. Ford walked up behind me and whispered in my ear—I'm going to use, exactly, the same language he did—'Frey,' he said, 'I'm tired of your fucking car. I'm going to approve it this afternoon, and it's your ass if it doesn't sell.' Of course it did sell. It sold and sold."

With the rear seat folded down, the Mustang fastback offered nearly as much cargo capacity as Plymouth's fastback Barracuda, though few buyers concerned themselves with the practical aspects of such sporty cars.

Ford designers tried to make the interior of the new Mustang as exciting as the exterior. Very little about the Mustang betrayed its econo-car origins.

In 1964, when the Mustang was introduced, a tachometer wasn't included as standard equipment. Ford marketers considered a low price to be one of the new car's critical features, and if owners wanted an extra like a tachometer, they usually installed it themselves.

Frey does not exaggerate. The car of which he speaks—the Mustang—did sell and sell. Ford introduced the Mustang as a 1964 1/2 model on April 17, 1964. By the end of that day Ford had sold over 22,000 Mustangs. By year's end it had sold 263,434 units, and by the end of the Mustang's first full year on the market Ford had sold 418,812 of the sporty 2+2 machines, an all-time sales record for the company.

In its most basic form, the Mustang represented little more than a Falcon with pretty sheet metal. In addition to its chassis, it shared its standard 170-cubic-inch, 101-horsepower inline six with the donor Falcon, but with its short trunk, long hood, and aggressive stance, it shared none of the Falcon's meek economy-car demeanor. When outfitted with one of the optional V-8 engines it had the berries to back up its good looks. The penny-pinching speed freak could opt for the F-code 260-cubic-inch V-8 engine from the Futura Sprint. In the Mustang, this mill was tuned to produce 164 horsepower, an acceptable output for the lightweight coupe, but the serious power junky opted for the 210-horsepower, 289-cubic-inch D-code engine, which made Frey's Mustang one quick car.

With the Mustang, Ford Motor had not just developed the perfect automobile for the emerging baby-boom market; it had developed the perfect automotive genre: the pony car. In its original form the pony car represented a fun, fast, sporty alternative to the

Although virtually non-existent today, vinyl-covered roofs were popular options on cars in the 1960s and 1970s. Their popularity declined during the 1980s, in part because styles changed and in part because they trapped moisture next to the metal roofs, causing corrosion.

With its long hood and short deck, the Ford Mustang redefined the proportions of a sporty car. From April 1964 forward, this would be the look that younger buyers demanded.

hairy-chested muscle car typified by cars like Pontiac's GTO. Still, Iacocca and company knew there was a market for hairy-chested muscle cars, and for 1965 they offered a couple of optional 289-cubic-inch engines that made the Mustang a bit hairier: the 225-horsepower A-code and the 271-horsepower K-code.

The K-code engine in particular had the Mustang nipping at the heels of the muscle car crowd. Its solid lifters, which needed periodic valve-lash adjustments, meant that an owner best be comfortable with grease-stained fingernails, but if a speed freak wanted a Mustang that would run with the new muscle cars coming from various GM divisions, the K-code was the only way to go.

When crunching the pony car formula, the math worked. The Mustang's success took just about everyone in the auto industry by surprise, including Henry Ford II. Before the Mustang had been on the market two full years, sales topped the one-million-unit mark. Compare that number to the fewer than 30,000 Sprints sold over roughly the same span of time and the answer to Lee Iacocca's rhetorical question—would the Falcon sell better if it looked better?—was clearly yes. Iacocca had been correct, the Deuce was wrong, and Frey's ass was safe.

CHEVY SICS A PANTHER ON FORD'S PONY

Initially, Chevrolet responded to the Mustang by doing what had worked in 1961—building a sportier version of the Corvair. The restyled 1965 Corvair was sportier, and by this time its flat-six could be ordered with a space-age turbocharger, giving it impressive acceleration for a six, but it was still a six. Some people within the company understood that this car would not be enough to attract the growing number of young buyers, and had been working on a concept similar to the Mustang since around the same time that Iacocca commissioned the Fairlane Committee.

Chevrolet's Design Vice President Bill Mitchell and Chief Designer Irv Rybicki began secretly working on their own pony car in 1962. Like the Mustang, the car used the underpinnings of an economy car as a starting point, in this case Chevrolet's Chevy II, and like the Mustang, the car featured a short rear deck and a long hood. The resulting clay mockup bore a remarkable resemblance to Ford's upcoming Mustang. "We didn't

Optional styled steel wheels were a $93.84 option and only available on V-8-powered cars.

Chevrolet's response to Ford's Mustang was the Camaro, introduced September 12, 1966.

If a buyer opted for both the RS and SS packages, the SS trim took precedence over the RS trim. Cars equipped with both the SS and RS packages featured grills with hidden headlights. This 1967 model has been painted a non-original shade of blue.

Chevrolet designers followed the already-classic pony-car proportions of Ford's Mustang—long hood, small passenger compartment, short deck— but managed to infuse the Camaro with enough of its own personality to avoid being considered derivative.

even know those devils at Ford were doing one," Rybicki says in Gary Witzenburg's book, *Camaro! From Challenger to Champion*.

Division Manager Bunkie Knudsen liked their concept car but worried that it would dilute a line of cars that was already being stretched thin. Chevrolet offered the Corvette sports car; the Corvair and Chevy II compacts; the full-sized Impala; and for 1964 was planning to introduce its version of the intermediate A-body chassis, the Chevelle. Add to that the bewildering array of sub models in production or development, like Monza, Nova, Malibu, Bel Air, and Caprice, and it's easy to see why Knudsen worried about adding another model to the mix.

Late the following year Hank Haga, chief of Chevrolet's Number Two Studio, developed a similar concept: the Super Nova. Mitchell and retired design vice president Harley Earl liked the car enough to develop a running prototype for the show car circuit. The public reacted well to the new car when it debuted at the World's Fair held in New York in early 1964, but GM's upper management was less enthusiastic. They wanted to maximize return on the money they had invested developing the Corvair and rightly feared that a car like Haga's would cannibalize Corvair sales. If the automotive status quo that existed at the time the Super Nova made its debut had remained the same, this decision might have been wise. But just a few short weeks after GM displayed the Super Nova, Iacocca, Frey, and company flipped the automotive status quo on its watery head with the new Mustang.

GM management was slow to accept the dramatically changing times. When the Mustang hit the market, most managers at General Motors were underwhelmed and didn't expect the new car to sell well. Some found the boxy styling and flat body panels old fashioned and unappealing, but more astute managers like Pete Estes knew the car would cause problems for General Motors.

As a young engineering student interning at Chevrolet, author Gary Witzenburg participated in a summer orientation meeting a few months after Ford brought out the Mustang and attended a lecture that featured Bill Mitchell as a speaker. In his book *Camaro!*, Witzenburg quotes Mitchell's response to the question "When will Chevy have an answer to the Mustang?"

"'We already have,' Mitchell bellowed. 'It's called the Corvair.'"

It was easy for GM's top executives to ignore the Mustang at first, because they existed in such rarified isolation that they genuinely didn't know that Ford was selling Mustangs faster than it could build them. They had been misinformed that the Mustang wasn't selling well, so when they learned that Ford had sold over 100,000 Mustangs in two months, it shook the hidebound corporation to its very core.

Even the most obtuse, self-absorbed corporate suit could not ignore the Mustang's numbers. The new pony car market Ford had created was just too lucrative for General Motors to remain on the sidelines. GM would have to swallow its corporate pride and admit that the Corvair could never be a player in this new pony car game. In August 1964, GM management finally gave Bunkie Knudsen official approval to develop Chevy's answer to the Mustang.

Given that the Mustang would have more than two years to develop a market and a reputation on the street, the new Chevy would have to be more than another good car; it would have to be better than the Mustang in every measure. It would have to be sportier, more comfortable, better looking, and most importantly, better performing. It would have to be quicker in a quarter-mile, have a faster top-end speed, and handle better than the Ford.

Given that the new car would be based on the lowly Chevy II platform, this would be a tall order for Chevy's engineers and designers. To improve on the Chevy II's less-than-stellar handling and noise and vibration isolation, Chevy engineers redesigned the unit-body chassis, focusing their efforts on the connection between the front subframe and the main body. They also modified the suspension extensively.

Unlike competitors Ford and Plymouth, which offered their pony cars in coupe, convertible, and fastback versions, Chevrolet only offered the Camaro as a coupe or convertible.

Internally, Chevrolet coded the car the F-body, perhaps a nod to the obvious fact that it had come into existence as a direct response to competitor Ford's pony car. The new Chevy needed to be in dealer showrooms as soon as possible to capture some of the Mustang's record-breaking sales, so Chevrolet engineers put in a lot of overtime to achieve all their design objectives in as short a time as possible.

In March 1966, just 18 months after official development began and before an official name had been chosen for the car, Chevrolet presented a fleet of 20 cars to the press. The press and public had already taken to calling the upcoming Chevrolet the Panther, though internally it was still called the F-body. This fleet of cars was the beginning of an unprecedented public relations blitz that led up to the official unveiling of Chevy's new pony car on September 12 of that year. The blitz worked, and the press and public were in a frothy lather by the time the car that Chevy called—after much internal debate—the Camaro hit the streets.

Technologically, the Camaro broke little new ground, but neither had the Mustang before it, and the lack of technical innovation hadn't hampered Mustang sales. For the most part, engine choices came from Chevrolet's existing stable of power plants, ranging from a 230-cubic-inch inline six that generated 140 horsepower to a 275-horsepower 327-cubic-inch V-8. Only one engine—the 350-cubic-inch small-block V-8—was unique to the Camaro.

General Motors Group Vice President Ed Cole, who had overseen the development of original Chevy small-block V-8 when he had been the general manager of Chevrolet a decade earlier, personally ordered engineer Don McPherson to bore out the 327 and create a 350-cubic-inch version of the venerable power plant. Unfortunately, the basic architecture of the block precluded such overboring and McPherson had to resort to increasing piston stroke, which created a number of additional challenges for McPherson's team of engineers. A longer stroke leads to higher peak piston speeds at a given rpm. A piston traveling up and down along a 3.48-inch stroke three thousand times each minute is moving a lot faster than a piston traveling along a 3.25-inch stroke during that same amount of time. Increased piston speeds lead to all kinds of engineering challenges, challenges McPherson and his team worked long hours to overcome.

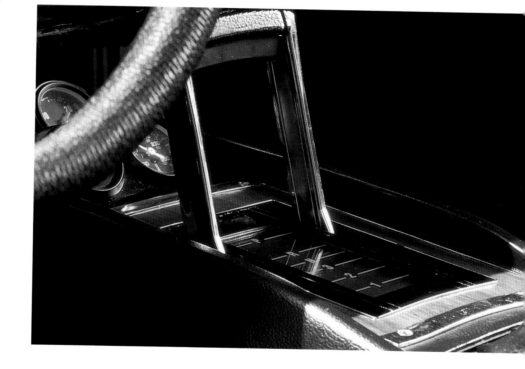

The planned introduction of the top-of-the-line Camaro SS 350, which would feature a high-output 295-horse version of the new engine, made McPherson's assignment even more challenging, but there seemed to be no choice but to develop a stronger engine. By 1965, as Camaro development was running at top speed, U.S. auto buyers had developed what seemed like an insatiable appetite for more and more power. A Camaro with a Nova-like SS trim package that was still powered by the same engines found in the pedestrian versions of the car would no longer cut it.

Chevrolet offered two optional automatic transmissions for the Camaro: the antiquated two-speed Powerglide and the vastly-better three-speed Turbo-Hydramatic.

GIVING THE PONY CAR SOME BEANS

The Camaro debuted to a generally positive response, but sales started off a bit slow. Overall reviewers liked the new car, though most agreed that it was no improvement over the Mustang. The SS version in particular was well received, even though the 350 engine suffered some early teething problems, but the Camaro was not the home run General Motors had hoped for. The primary reason was that in the Mustang, Chevy had taken a shot at a moving target. In most respects the Camaro represented an improvement, however slight, over the 1964 1/2 Mustang. If the Camaro had debuted at the same time as Ford's Mustang 2 1/2 years earlier, it may have been the defining automobile of the baby-boom generation. But the Camaro was not competing against that earlier Mustang; it was competing against a redesigned 1967 Mustang. The new Mustang had more contemporary styling, more features, and most importantly, a new engine: the big-block 390.

While Ford's advanced thin-wall casting technique had resulted in a lightweight V-8 engine that fit within the tight confines of the Falcon engine bay, its big-block engines were still large and heavy and needed a lot of space in any engine bay in which they might reside. Fitting one of the beasts in a 1964 1/2 to 1966 Mustang was out of the question, so for the 1967 model year Ford designers widened the Mustang by more than 2.5 inches, opening up just enough space in the engine bay to drop a big-block V-8. And, of course, this is exactly what they did. For an additional $232 a buyer could order a 320-horsepower 390-cubic-inch big-block and transform his pony car into a genuine muscle car. While the new mill only generated 25 more horsepower than the Camaro's small-block 350, it pumped out excessive torque, the twisting force that made exiting a drive-in a much more impressive event than did peak horsepower.

Clearly excessive power and torque sold cars. In 1967, Chevrolet sold 220,906 Camaros, enough to make the car profitable for the division but well short of the projected 300,000 unit sales. Meanwhile, Ford sold more than two Mustangs for every Camaro sold by Chevrolet. Making the Mustang bigger and badder had been a good move. By this time America had entered an era of excess. Excess defined every aspect of life in the United States, both public and private. Americans had excessive appetites and excessive income with which to feed those appetites. The biggest bulge of the baby boom—what sociologists call the pig in the python—were in their late teens and early twenties, a time of life when hormones play a much larger role in decision making than restraint and common sense. By 1967 they had formed the most indulgent society since the heyday of ancient Rome. They indulged in excessive artistic expression, excessive sexual activity,

In 1967, Chevrolet introduced a new small-block V-8 at the same time as the new Camaro pony car: the 350. This engine, created by lengthening the stroke of the 327-cubic-inch engine, was standard equipment on the SS Camaro.

and excessive abuse of mood-altering substances. Their love of excessive cars with excessive engines capable of attaining excessive speeds fit in perfectly with their fast-paced sex-drugs-and-rock-and-roll lifestyles.

If the Camaro was to compete in this atmosphere of excess, it too would have to feature an excessively large engine. A couple of months after unveiling the car, Chevrolet engineers gave the Camaro exactly that. Like the Chevelle before it, the Camaro received the division's Mark IV engine, a 396-cubic-inch, 325-horsepower street-going version of Chevrolet's awe-inspiring 427-cubic-inch Mark II racing motor, as a $263.30 option. If an owner was willing to deal with the hassle of mechanical lifters instead of hydraulic lifters and had the financial means to shell out an additional $237, he could get the 375-horsepower L78 version of the engine. Like the 390-cubic-inch rendition of the Mustang, the 396-cubic-inch version of the Camaro pushed Chevy's pony car squarely into the muscle car ranks.

When Chevrolet introduced the Camaro as a competitor for Ford's Mustang in 1967, it aimed at a moving target—that same year Ford introduced a redesigned Mustang with a wider engine bay that could accommodate Ford's 390-cubic-inch big-block engine.

For the 1967 model year, Ford designers widened the Mustang by more than 2.5 inches, opening just enough space to drop a big-block V-8 in the engine bay.

In 1967, the car-buying public demanded excess, and Chevrolet responded by making the 396-cubic-inch, Mark IV engine available in the Camaro. When buyers chose the optional 375-horsepower L78 version, Mustang owners could only watch the Camaro's disappearing taillights.

The 390-cubic-inch, FE-series engine offered as an option for the 1967 Mustang produced 320 horsepower, enough to make the Mustang a true muscle car.

PLYMOUTH'S PONY FISH

If the Mustang was the undisputed champion of the pony car market and the Camaro its up-and-coming challenger, then Plymouth's Barracuda was its sad clown. From the timing of the car's introduction, just two weeks before Ford dropped its atomic-bomb Mustang into the market, things had not rolled the Barracuda's way. Unlike the Mustang and later Camaro, the Barracuda's humble economy-car origins were clearly evident in the car's sheet metal and shape. Though its optional small-block V-8 engine held huge potential, its initial output of 180 horsepower put its performance more in the league of the Falcon Futura Sprint than the 271-horsepower Mustang. Its massive glass fastback design gave it a class-leading 23.7 cubic feet of cargo capacity when the rear seatback was folded down, but this feature failed to stir the average baby boomer's automotive libido. The Mustang outsold the Barracuda by a more than five-to-one ratio.

The one area where Plymouth's new fish outshone the competition was handling. Chrysler's unique torsion-bar front suspension helped give the compact Barracuda excellent ride and handling characteristics. These attributes would be put to good use on racetracks in coming years. Chrysler engineer Scott Harvey was an accomplished amateur road and rally racer, and his experience and expertise showed in the Barracuda's chassis design.

In 1965 Plymouth tried to make the Barracuda more competitive with the Mustang and introduced a sportier Formula S version of its little fish. The Formula S capitalized on the Barracuda's strength—handling—and improved its weaknesses. Harvey used his racing Barracuda as a test bed for developing performance-enhancing features like quicker-geared steering, improved transmission ratios, better shocks and springs, and most importantly, the Commando 273 version of the small-block V-8. With its four-barrel carburetor, dual exhaust, dual-point distributor, high-lift camshaft, and 10.5:1 compression ratio, the little engine's power output rose from 180 to 235 horsepower. This put the Barracuda slightly above the A-code version of Ford's 289-cubic-inch Mustang.

While the Barracuda's performance was on par with the Mustang, its looks weren't. Of the Formula S, *Road & Track* wrote, "For those people who enjoy sports car driving but, for reasons of family or business, need four seats and adequate baggage space, the

If the Camaro SS buyer was willing to spend an additional $263 for the optional big-block engine, he had 325 horsepower at his disposal—enough to reduce a pair of skinny 70-series bias-ply tires to molten rubber.

The 396-cubic-inch engine returned for the 1968 model year. Buyers who didn't mind adjusting valves could order the solid-lifter L78 version , which produced 375 horsepower.

In 1969 a Camaro SS paced the 500-mile race at the Indianapolis Motor Speedway. Naturally, Chevrolet produced a commemorative edition for public consumption.

Barracuda would certainly make an excellent compromise." Excellent or not, the members of the sex-drugs-and-rock-and-roll generation were in no mood to compromise. They were more interested in the Mustang's flash than the Barracuda's virtues. With the help of the sporty Formula S, Plymouth sold 65,596 Barracudas for 1965, making it the top-selling model in Plymouth's lineup that year. But for the 1965 model year Ford sold 559,451 Mustangs. In an attempt to capture some of the Mustang's sales, Plymouth revamped the Barracuda for 1966, giving it a restyled interior, a new instrument panel with a 150-mile-per-hour speedometer, and optional front disc brakes. But by this time the car's Valiant-based styling was looking even more dated than in previous years and sales plummeted 42 percent, to 38,029 cars. Meanwhile Ford sold an astonishing 607,568 Mustangs for the 1966 model year.

At this point, Chrysler made the decision to develop a distinct pony car, internally coded the E-body. While this program would eventually yield the most outrageous pony cars of all time—the Plymouth 'Cuda and Dodge Challenger—it would be several years before these cars hit the market. In the meantime, Plymouth would have to have an interim car to compete with the Mustang and the upcoming General Motors F-cars.

When Plymouth redesigned its Barracuda for the 1967 model year, it again included a fastback model in the lineup. While this curvaceous new body was much sexier than the old Valiant-based Barracuda, it still did not possess the sex appeal of the Mustang.

When Plymouth restyled the Barracuda for 1967, it offered coupe and convertible versions in addition to the fastback.

THE FISH GETS TEETH

In November 1966, Plymouth introduced a dramatically redesigned Barracuda, available as a coupe, a fastback, or a convertible—the same body configurations as the rival Mustang. With its curvaceous bodywork, the Barracuda finally broke away from its economy-car roots. Mechanically the new car was even further removed from its Valiant ancestor. Both versions of the 273 engine returned for 1967—the 180-horsepower standard version and the 235-horsepower Commando version—but the big news was the inclusion of a

big-block V-8 engine option. With some clever packaging that included the mandatory deletion of air conditioning, power steering, and power brakes, Chrysler's engineers had managed to stuff a 383 B-block engine between the front wheels of the Formula S version of the little Barracuda. Restrictive exhaust headers necessitated by the lack of space in the engine compartment limited total horsepower output to 280. Peak horsepower may have been less than its big-block competition, but a massive 400 ft-lb of torque made the 383-equipped Formula S a burn-out champion. When the 383 option was checked on the order sheet, front disc brakes were automatically included as part of the option. The 10-inch drum brakes found on the pedestrian versions of the Barracuda would not suffice for a car with the performance potential of the Formula S.

For 1968, Chrysler's engineers upped the power output of the 383-cubic-inch engine to an even 300, but the real news was a new small-block, the 340. While this engine shared the same basic engineering as the smaller members of the LA series of motors, the 340

Although a handsomely styled car, the 1967 Barracuda still featured the mid-cockpit proportions of a miniature sedan rather than the long hood and short deck of a pony car.

featured more efficient cylinder heads with better flow characteristics and huge 2.02-inch valves. While only rated at 275 horsepower, the high-revving, overachieving small-block cranked out an impressive 340 ft-lb of torque. This made 340-equipped cars some of the most entertaining vehicles of the muscle car era, easily capable of running with the big-block competition. The weight the big-block engine placed over the front tires had not done much to help the Formula S maintain the handling reputation developed by earlier Barracudas. Mounting the lightweight 340 small-block in the engine bay helped bring balanced handling back to the Barracuda nameplate.

Though it was one of the most balanced and best performing cars of the era, the original Barracuda never made much of a mark in the automotive world. It suffered from being the rear-guard camp follower of the early pony car era, a day late and a dollar short of marketing trends of the time. This would not change until Chrysler introduced the E-body series for 1970.

PONTIAC'S F-BODY

Midway through development of its upcoming F-car, GM management decided Pontiac should build its own version of the platform. John DeLorean, who had succeeded Pete Estes as manager of Pontiac Division, had been trying to get a European-style, lightweight, two-seat sports car approved for several years. In his book *Firebird! America's Premier Performance Car*, author Gary Witzenburg describes the event that led to DeLorean's sports-car project morphing into a Pontiac F-car:

Though a bit conservative on the outside, the 1967 Barracuda interior was every bit as sporty as its competition from Ford and General Motors.

> By March (1966), DeLorean's persistence was beginning to try the patience of GM president (James) Roche and executive vice president Ed Cole. One day, according to one of the designers involved, "he made a big pitch to Ed Cole, and they had a row in the studio. John as much as called Cole a bunch of rude names. They turned around at that point and Cole said, 'Well, you can take the Camaro and make a car out of that. End of discussion.'

The corporate mother ship wanted Pontiac to release its version of the F-car in the fall of 1966, at the same time as Chevrolet released the Camaro, but that would not be possible

unless Pontiac simply rebadged a version of the Chevy. DeLorean insisted that his division's F-car be uniquely Pontiac and not simply a rehashed Chevrolet. He arranged for a six-month delay in the introduction of Pontiac's interpretation of the F-car.

Jim Wangers considered the delay an opportunity to correct some of the Camaro's shortcomings. In *Glory Days*, Wangers writes, "The Camaro, frankly, was not an improved package over the Mustang. . . . Ford had already established the genre and Chevrolet had failed to break any new ground."

Chevrolet had already released a small fleet of preproduction cars to select members of the press by the time Pontiac engineers even began working on the car, so the basic design was finalized for all practical purposes. The Pontiac division didn't have a lot of options for making its version of the F-car unique, given the advanced state of development of the Camaro and the short amount of time available, even with a six-month extension. Reshaping sheet metal was out of the question, so Pontiac designers were relegated to reshaping the nose and tail sections of the car.

In 1968, Chrysler introduced a much-improved version of its LA-series small-block V-8. This 340-cubic-inch motor featured improved cylinder heads with bigger valves and produced a respectable 340 ft-lb of torque.

Pontiac's John DeLorean wanted to build a European-style, two-seat sports car, but GM management felt such a car would cannibalize Corvette sales. Instead, they ordered Pontiac to produce a version of Chevrolet's Camaro: the Firebird.

The top model in Pontiac's 1967 Firebird lineup was the Firebird 400, featuring a version of the engine that powered the GTO muscle car.

DeLorean thought the Camaro looked too tall and ungainly, so he had the Pontiac F-car lowered by an inch and insisted that all Pontiac F-cars roll on Firestone's new 70-series Wide-Oval tires. This gave the Pontiac a harsher ride than the Camaro, but it also gave the new pony car a much more aggressive stance.

Pontiac used most of the limited time available in an attempt to improve the Camaro's suspension. Pontiac engineers did not believe that the Camaro's handling was up to Pontiac standards. In *Firebird!*, Witzenburg quotes Steve Malone, who had assumed chief engineer duties after DeLorean had been promoted to division manager: "I remember (the Camaro) was a real basket case when we got it, and we spent four or five months trying to make (its handling) acceptable by our standards."

The rear suspension received the bulk of Pontiac engineers' attention. Chevrolet had used a pair of single-leaf tapered springs to suspend the rear axle. This reduced manufacturing costs dramatically but reduced the ability to tune the rear suspension in equal measure. Pontiac developed a more-expensive multileaf spring that allowed variable spring ratios in its F-car, but these weren't ready in time for the car's debut in early 1967. The more advanced multileaf springs didn't appear until the advent of the 1968 model.

Pontiac's chassis engineers made a number of other suspension changes to address the ferocious wheel hop the Camaro experienced under acceleration, and to a lesser degree

under braking. By the time the Pontiac F-car went on sale, division engineers had installed an adjustable radius rod on all but the base model (Pontiac used a pair of rods on the high-performance models). This helped tame the rear end somewhat, but Pontiac had a more effective cure under development. Using a staggered-shock arrangement, with the passenger-side shock ahead of the rear axle and the driver-side shock behind it, prevented the axle from rotating, largely eliminating the tendency of the axle to hop under stress. Like the multileaf springs, this design would not be ready in time for the initial car's debut but would appear on the 1968 model. Except for the addition of radius rods, 1967 Pontiac F-cars had to make due with the Camaro's econocar rear suspension design.

In addition to handling better, DeLorean wanted the Pontiac F-car, which would ultimately be named Firebird, to feature a selection of engines unique to the Pontiac. These ranged from an advanced inline-six-cylinder to the big GTO engine, which by that time had grown to 400 cubic inches.

Pontiac offered optional hood-mounted tachometers on both the GTO and the Firebird.

As with other models, Pontiac
positioned the Firebird as a more
upscale version of its corporate sister
from rival GM division, Chevrolet.

Technologically, the economical six-cylinder power plant, which featured an advanced overhead cam (OHC) design, was the most interesting of the group. The engine had first appeared in the 1966 Tempest, but Pontiac had developed it as a potential engine for its hoped-for two-seat sports car. High-revving OHC six-cylinders were the power plants of choice for lightweight European sports cars such as those built buy Jaguar and Triumph, the Pontiac's intended competition, and Pontiac's advanced design had the potential to compete with the best of them. The version of the 230-cubic-inch engine mounted in the basic Firebird coupe used a one-barrel Rochester carburetor to develop a respectable 165 horsepower, as much as the small-block V-8s of just a few years earlier. If a buyer wanted

Pontiac didn't begin developing the Firebird until the Camaro was almost ready for production. As a result, the 1967 model was more similar to the Camaro than later models.

In 1968, Pontiac incorporated a number of chassis improvements designed to tame the rear wheel hop that plagued the Camaro under hard acceleration and braking.

Pontiac built several Grand Marque Firebirds for the show circuit in 1968.

to fork over an extra $105.60, he or she could upgrade to a Sprint model of the Firebird, which featured a high-output version of the high-revving engine. This engine used all the standard hot-rodder tricks—four-barrel carburetor, higher compression, hotter cams, larger valves, freer breathing intake and exhaust systems—to develop 215 horsepower. When mated to a Muncie four-speed transmission, this hyper-high-performance package provided enough power to push the 3,300-pound coupe through the quarter-mile in the low-17-second bracket.

With the Firebird Sprint Pontiac had produced a world-class sporty car, but the model failed to strike a chord with the buying public. "Without a doubt, the Firebird OHC six Sprint package was one of the best balanced performance cars Pontiac ever built," Jim Wangers writes in *Glory Days*. "Nimble and quick, the Firebird Sprint was never truly appreciated by a market enamored by the V-8 engine." Pontiac was trying to provide a balanced car to a youth market drunk on excess. To such buyers, "balance" was another word for compromise, and as mentioned before, the baby boomers chose excess and extremes over balance and compromise every time.

To give the Firebird a more aggressive stance than the Camaro, Pontiac engineers lowered the suspension by 1 inch and fitted Firestone's new 70-series Wide-Oval tires.

With a four-speed transmission and a 400-cubic-inch engine—conservatively rated at 325 horsepower—the Firebird 400 was capable of quarter-mile times in the 15-second range.

American Motors got into the pony car market with its Javelin, introduced for the 1968 model year. In the middle of the 1969 model year, AMC offered a series of psychedelic "Big Bad" colors, like Big Bad Blue covering this SST model.

From the start Pontiac knew its customers would choose excess over balance, and the Firebird offered a number of engines to satiate buyers' hedonistic cravings for excess power. Beginning with a two-barrel version of the division's 326-cubic-inch engine, which generated 250 horsepower and 333 ft-lb of torque, buyers could move up to a series of increasingly potent V-8s. The H.O. version of the 326 used dual-exhaust, a four-barrel carburetor, and higher-compression to achieve 285 horsepower and 359 ft-lb of torque, but for a public that preferred extremes, the engine of choice was the 400. For this engine Pontiac developed a high-end package worthy of the power plant: the Firebird 400.

The Firebird 400 made the suits at GM headquarters nervous. They had given up trying to enforce the old 10-pounds-per-cubic-inch rule, but the thought of mounting the

powerful GTO engine in such a small car made them go moist with fear. Strong GTO sales had forced General Motors to back away from the old 10-pounds-per-cubic-inch rule. In an attempt to reassert its misguided authority, GM management changed the rule to limit cars to one horsepower for every ten pounds. They also banned the use of multiple carburetors on passenger cars at this time. As a result of this futile, unilateral attempt to quash the horsepower wars raging in Detroit, the corporate mother ship ordered Pontiac to detune the 400-cubic-inch engine for use in the Firebird.

Pontiac rated both the standard 400 and the version equipped with the optional Ram Air functional hood scoop at 325 horsepower. In part, this relatively low rating was the result of a half-hearted attempt to detune the engine, a token act that consisted of such easily disabled pieces as a tab on the carburetor linkage that prevented the throttle from

For 1970, AMC designers tweaked the sheet metal of the Javelin in an attempt to improve sales. To further improve sales, AMC offered a Mark Donohue version to commemorate Donohue's Trans-Am racing effort.

In 1969, AMC offered street-going replicas of its Trans-Am racers, but sales of the cars, which featured loud, red-white-and-blue paint schemes, were slow. The 1970 Mark Donohue editions were available in any color AMC offered and sales were much stronger.

opening fully. Simply breaking off the tab unleashed an additional 25 horsepower. But there was more to this low rating than a token attempt to placate corporate safetycrats. In part, the 325-horsepower rating was fictitious. Pontiac purposely underrated the 400-cubic-inch power plant to avoid frightening the timid souls running General Motors and their equally mousy counterparts in the insurance industry, and also to avoid pissing off GTO drivers. These folks preferred to think of their muscle cars as superior to the new breed of pony cars, and a Firebird with a horsepower rating identical to that of a GTO would make it difficult for the GTO drivers to maintain that illusion.

Underrated or not, the new Firebird 400 hauled ass.

A bone stock Firebird 400 could slip below the 15-second bracket at the drag strip and a mildly tweaked example could easily break into the 12-second bracket. Even if buyers had no intention of racing their Firebird 400s, they could impress their friends with big, smoky burn-outs. The engine's 410 ft-lb of torque meant that such antics were merely a mashing of the accelerator away.

Pontiac came late to the pony car party, but it had done its homework. It had learned from the mistakes of its predecessors and had made the car as right as possible from the start. Within a few months, the division would excise most of the Camaro's ill handling with the introduction of an improved rear suspension, but even without such improvements, the Firebird 400 was a true muscle car straight out of the box. First-year sales of more than 80,000 units—an impressive number given the car's February 1967 introduction—indicated that the Firebird was just the car the baby-boom market wanted. Used to being a distant third to Chevrolet and Ford, Pontiac found itself nipping at the heels of its more prolific competitors in the pony car market.

THE REDHEADED STEPCHILD

The new pony car market proved so lucrative that it even attracted the attention of American Motors Corporation. The redheaded stepchild of the American auto industry, AMC had stayed in business while other small U.S. automakers like Studebaker and Packard went teats-up primarily on the success of its economical Rambler line of cars. AMC had unwittingly almost invented the pony car a decade earlier when it had dropped its then-new 327-cubic-inc OHV V-8 into a Rambler and called it a Rebel. This 255-horsepower engine made the lightweight Rambler Rebel the second-fastest car built in America, bested only by Chevrolet's potent fuel-injected Corvette. Had the Rambler been blessed with one iota of the style of Chevy's 'Vette, the car may well have changed automotive history. Unfortunately for AMC, the car looked like the same toady Rambler your weird bachelor uncle drove to the Elks club every Tuesday night. It was not the stuff of which legends are made, and after a limited production run of 1,500 units the sad-looking little car motored off into the sunset.

American Motors limped into the 1960s selling economical Ramblers to the Vicks-Vapo-Rub-and-hemorrhoid-pillow crowd, but in marketing surveys the emerging youth market was most likely to respond to a question about the Rambler with: "Do they still make those?" Homely economy might have been enough to keep the company alive in the past, but by the time Ford introduced its Mustang, AMC cars were under serious pressure from the competition. Not only had the domestic competition gotten into the small car act with cars like the Falcon, Chevy II, Corvair, and Valiant, but automakers

All the Mark Donohue Javelins were supposed to feature the full-boat SST package, which consisted of "antelope-grain" vinyl bucket seats and a counsel with a floor-mounted shifter; some apparently escaped the factory with column-mounted shifters.

from Germany and Japan were importing increasingly popular cars. American Motors found itself in a position where it had to evolve, and evolve quickly, or face extinction. By 1965, AMC was losing money and in serious danger of going out of business. In the spring of 1966, about the same time as Cole told DeLorean to stuff his two-seat concept car and build a Pontiac version of the Camaro, AMC finally approved the development of a car that would become the 1968 Javelin.

Designing a car for the youth market would be a Herculean task for AMC designers. They had the talent to craft a car that had the sporty looks the baby boomers craved, but providing sporty performance would be difficult using the engines AMC had in its stable. The only V-8 engine the company built at the time had been designed in the mid-1950s, and its antiquated technology made it an implausible choice for performance tuning. Any serious attempt to turn around AMC's fortunes would require a modern V-8 engine, so a team headed by engineer Dave Potter began working on a lightweight V-8 that used state-of-the-art thin-wall casting technology.

The engine design Potter and his team developed had serious performance potential. When introduced halfway through 1966 it displaced 290 cubic inches and generated 225 horsepower when equipped with a four-barrel carburetor, but the smooth-running lightweight power plant had the potential to produce much more than that. The engine debuted in the AMC Rogue, a sporty version of the Rambler American compact. Because the venerable Rambler name had negative connotations for the youth market, this sporty version of the American was not called a Rambler. Had the Rogue debuted five years earlier, it might have been able to compete against the likes of the Chevy II Nova SS and the Falcon Futura Sprint, but by the summer of 1966 it was competing against the established Mustang and the soon-to-be-released Chevrolet Camaro. Sales amounted to about a quarter of the sales of Plymouth's slow-selling Barracuda and less than two-tenths of one percent of Mustang sales.

While cars like the Rogue and the 1967 Super American did not make enough of an impression on the market to remind baby boomers that AMC was still in business, they did serve as test beds for developing the new V-8 engine. By the time the 1968 cars were made available to the public, the engine had grown into a 390-cubic-inch torque monster. While the engine only generated 315 peak horsepower, it produced a class-leading 425 ft-lb of torque. The torque-heavy nature of the engine may have been due to the fact that AMC management, which still harbored prejudice toward performance cars and the youth market in general, originally intended to offer the engine only in its large Ambassador sedan as part of an optional towing package.

Ultimately, greed overcame management's prejudices and the engine was made available in AMC's new-for-1968 pony car, the Javelin. The new car, introduced on September 26, 1967, shared a few basic drivetrain and suspension bits with the lowly Rambler American, but the unit-body structure was much stiffer, to better handle the 390's prodigious torque, though that optional engine was not available when the car was first introduced. Initially, the top engine offered was a 280-horsepower 343-cubic-inch V-8 with a four-barrel carburetor and dual exhaust. To appeal to the youth market, AMC offered a sportier trim package, the SST. The SST consisted of additional pieces of trim and high-back bucket

In 1971, AMC redesigned the Javelin, making the AMX an option for the car rather than its own model.

In the middle of the 1968 model year AMC introduced the most radical new American car since the 1955 Thunderbird: the two-seat AMX. This 1969 1/2 model is painted Big Bad Green.

seats; there was nothing in the package to contribute to the car's performance. For that, a potential owner would have to order the "Go" package. In addition to the high-output 343 V-8, this package included power front disc brakes, wide-profile tires, front anti-sway bar, heavy-duty springs and shocks, and, of course, a sporty racing stripe.

In February 1968, AMC finally made the 390-cubic-inch version of the engine available as an option for the Javelin. The addition of this engine elevated the Javelin to the status of muscle car. When equipped with a four-speed transmission, a stock 390 Javelin could

break the 15-second barrier in the quarter-mile, making it one of the fastest cars on the market. Like Pontiac with its Super Duty program, AMC offered a wide assortment of performance parts from its parts catalog. Unlike Pontiac, which had instituted its Super Duty program in part due to corporate pride, AMC offered its "Group 19" parts (named after the section of the AMC parts catalog in which they appeared) due to necessity. Because the V-8 engine was such a new design and because AMC's market share was so low, the aftermarket hadn't developed a lot of performance parts for AMC cars. AMC had no option other than to develop its own line of performance parts if it wanted to sell cars to the hot-rod market.

The Javelin earned a profit for AMC, but the company had hoped to sell more than the 56,462 units it sold for the 1968 model year. American Motors needed a car that would do more than turn a profit. It needed a car that would build a high-performance reputation. It needed more than a pony car—it needed a true sports car. In February 1968, the same time the 390 engine became available in the Javelin, it got just that.

For all practical purposes, the AMX is a Javelin with twelve inches excised from its mid section, eliminating its rear seat area.

The 390-cubic-inch engine in the AMX produced an impressive 425 ft-lb of torque, making the relatively lightweight two-seater a formidable opponent in a stoplight drag race.

This is one of an unknown number of California 500 Specials built in 1969. This example features a rare set of optional dealer-installed Trendsetter Sidewinder sidepipes.

TWO-PLUS-NOTHING

By 1966 American Motors needed to take drastic measures to stay in business. That year the company lost $12.6 million dollars and its sales declined 12 percent. The company's earlier attempt at building a car for the youth market—the Rambler Marlin introduced for the 1965 model year—had tanked. The person responsible for the fiasco, AMC President Roy Abernathy, soon found himself in an unemployment line, where he had a number of other former AMC top executives and board members to keep him company. All of the AMC brass who had suddenly found themselves lacking gainful employment had dug in their

The two-seat AMX was built to attract attention to struggling American Motors Corporation, and it did that, but it never sold in huge numbers. After the 1970 model year, the two-seat AMX disappeared and the AMX nameplate became an option package on the four-seat Javelin.

Carroll Shelby built and sold his own hybrid muscle car/sports car, the 427 Cobra, created by mounting a monstrous Ford NASCAR racing engine in a lightweight English sports car body.

heels and resisted building a sporty small car for baby boomers. Those who remained would make no such mistake. In fact, they were willing to go to the opposite extreme.

In a last ditch effort to save the company and their jobs, AMC's top management decided to build a car completely unlike the proletarian economy cars that had been the company's cash cows in the past. In September 1966, AMC designers began developing the AMX, an all-out sports car. Or rather, an all-out personal sports-luxury car, like the original two-seat Thunderbird.

The company didn't have the resources to develop a true sports car, which would have required a sophisticated suspension and exotic lightweight materials. It barely had the funds to develop the Javelin sports coupe that would have to serve as the fundament upon which the new AMX two-seater would be built. For all practical purposes, the AMX would have to be a Javelin with 12 inches removed from its floorpan. Except for slightly reshaped body panels, every Javelin part from the front seats and forward, including the drivetrain, would be used in the AMX, including doors, door panels, dash, gauges, windshield, steering column, firewall, fenders, and pretty much every other part.

The AMX was a long shot for struggling American Motors, but in most ways it succeeded. Thanks primarily to lighter weight and upgraded suspension components, the AMX performed measurably better than its Javelin counterpart. American Motors sold just 19,134 two-seat AMX models during the car's three-year production run, but the car had been built to serve a higher purpose than just generating sales. It had been designed as a much-needed halo car, one that would attract the attention of baby boomers and help shed the Rambler image that was suffocating the company in a youth-oriented marketplace. Toward that end, the AMX succeeded.

The heart of the 427 Cobra was its 427 Ford NASCAR racing engine, nicknamed the "side-oiler" because it featured oil passages machined into the sides of the engine block.

PONY RACING

It didn't take the Total Performance folks at Ford long to realize that their newly invented pony car had racing potential, and not just at NHRA drag strips and NASCAR oval tracks. The new Mustang had the hidden potential to go road racing as well.

But early testing indicated that any road racing potential might be hidden a bit too well. When Ford engineer Joe Mulholland first decided to take the Mustang racing in the summer of 1964, he, Ford product planner Joe Onken, and Australian racer Allan Moffat took a couple of production notchbacks to a tight (13 turns in 1.5 miles) road course for some testing. As Onken recalls, the two cars went off the road everywhere. By the end of the day, both cars were completely spent.

To create a competitive racing car from its new Mustang, Ford enlisted former-racer and auto builder Carroll Shelby. The car Shelby created, the 1965 Shelby GT350, was a true race car, barely civilized for street use.

If the Mustang was to be anything but a joke on a racetrack, it needed serious help. Onken went to Don Frey and outlined the problems he faced. Frey proposed an inspired solution: bring in Carroll Shelby on the project. Shelby had already been building his own home-rolled muscle cars, the 427 Cobras, small English sports cars powered by Ford's all-conquering 427 NASCAR engine. These cars were sold through select Ford dealerships and even though they didn't sell in huge numbers, dealers liked having Cobras on their showroom floors because they generated excitement and brought in customers. This endeared Shelby to Ford boss Lee Iacocca, and Frey thought he would be the best choice for converting a Mustang into a race car. Besides, Shelby owed Ford a favor. The company had been selling him Cobra engines at a loss and Frey thought it might be time for the ex-racer from Texas to give something back to the company.

"He turned that little English sports car into a race winner," Frey told Onken. "He's beating Ferrari in Europe. Maybe it's time to call Mr. Shelby in to repay the favor we've given him with his Cobra engines."

The initial plan called for Shelby to build 100 Mustang-based race cars. Shelby and Phil Remington, Shelby's head development mechanic, scoured Ford's special parts catalog, finding items for police cars and NASCAR racers that would turn Ford's wallowing "secretary's car," as Shelby called the Mustang, into a competitive racer.

Shelby's engineering team tightened up the front suspension to prevent the front tires from rolling under the car in hard cornering. In the back they installed different springs and drag-type traction bars that required cutting slots through the floorpan so the long bars could be mounted inside the cab. This required removing the rear seats, but the seats had to be removed anyway for the car to comply with SCCA (Sports Car Club of America) racing regulations. Shelby commandeered heavy-duty brakes and a heavy-duty rear axle from Ford's station-wagon towing package. His team gutted the interior, removing everything possible to save

The Shelby GT350 featured racing accoutrements, such as a pinned hood, for a reason—the car was practically track ready as delivered.

Along with the GT350 street cars, Shelby built 36 GT350R racers. These cars featured 289-cubic-inch engines tuned to produce 350 to 360 horsepower.

The racing version of the 1965 Shelby Mustang, the GT350R, was stripped of all street-going equipment, including the front and rear bumpers.

Because the GT350R was a pure race car never meant to be licensed for street use, it needed no silencing mufflers for its exhaust pipes. Earplugs were required to prevent serious hearing loss.

The GT350R was as purposeful inside as out. All an owner needed to go racing was a helmet, a fireproof suit, and a lot of high-octane gasoline.

Shelby replaced the glass in the rear window and doors with Plexiglas to save weight in the GT350Rs.

The 36 cars Shelby built as racers came from Ford without gas tanks. Shelby created large-capacity tanks for the cars by slicing Mustang fuel tanks in half, then welding them up.

In 1966, Shelby sold Hertz Rent-A-Car 1,000 Shelby GT350s for the company's rental fleet. These cars were more civilized than the racers-with-license-plates Shelby sold in 1965, but they were still among the wildest cars in any rental fleet.

weight. Toward that same end, they removed the rear bumper and replaced the steel front bumper with a fiberglass piece. They also replaced the glass rear window with a Plexiglas unit.

Shelby's team decided to give the Mustang an alphanumeric name. They settled on "GT350," not because of the 350–360 horsepower the racing motor generated, but for a more arbitrary reason. Unable to decide upon a name, Shelby had Remington pace off the distance between his company's conference room and the shop, which happened to be about 350 feet.

Shelby built 36 cars to these racing specifications, and another 100 less-austere cars with bumpers for the street to make the car eligible for SCCA racing. These cars featured more amenities inside, along with K-code motors tweaked to produce 306 horsepower.

After the initial run of 100 street racers, Shelby began to tone down the road-going versions of the GT350. He'd learned an important fact about baby boomers and their relationships to their cars—they thought they wanted to own race cars until they actually owned race cars. Then they realized that what they really wanted were quiet, comfortable cars that looked like racers.

TRANS-AMERICAN SEDAN CHAMPIONSHIP

In 1966, the SCCA began running a road-racing series that would prove the ideal arena in which the new pony cars could compete. This series featured sedans with four permanent seats competing in two classes: an amateur class and a professional class. A series of regional races comprised the amateur class, culminating with the top three finishers from six separate regions competing in the American Road Race of Champions (ARRC). The professional races consisted of longer events, called the Trans-American Sedan Championship, or Trans-Am races.

This series would have a tremendous effect on the development of production cars, because in addition to awarding a championship to the winning driver at the end of a season, it awarded a championship to the winning manufacturer. This made competing in the series an attractive marketing proposition for U.S. automakers trying to sell pony cars to baby boomers, and in 1966 every manufacturer was either selling or developing such a pony car. The SCCA enforced strict rules in the Trans-Am series, rules intended to keep the cars on the tracks as close as possible to the cars manufactured for street use. This

Chevrolet's offering for SCCA Trans-Am racing was the Z/28 Camaro. Shown is a 1969 model.

Developed by Chevrolet racing czar Vince Piggins, the 1967 Z/28 used some of the improved suspension pieces Pontiac was developing for the upcoming Firebird.

made the series extremely popular with fans across the United States right from the initial series of seven races, and the popularity of the series increased throughout the 1960s.

The predictable result was that every new pony car introduced from 1966 on would include a model or option package designed to homologate the car for Trans-Am racing. Plymouth developed the Formula S version of its Barracuda into a competitive Trans-Am racer and even struggling American Motors got into the act with its Javelin. Before Chevy's pony car entrant even hit the market, the Bowtie division had begun developing a Trans-Am homologation package for its Camaro.

OPTION PACKAGE 28

At Chevrolet, Vince Piggins managed a department called "product promotion." This was really code for "racing department," a deception necessitated by the fact that General Motors had not followed Ford's lead and told the AMA to self-fornicate with its racing ban. Quite the opposite: General Motors had instituted an internal racing ban even more Draconian than the AMA ban, but that ban had been created in response to the threat of federal trust busting against GM. By 1966, it was clear that GM was not going to gain 60 percent of the U.S. auto market. If anything, GM was losing market share to Ford, thanks in large part to the phenomenal sales success of the Mustang. General Motors corporate management had began to unbunch its undies a bit regarding its racing ban, but Pete Estes and his Chevrolet division still felt it wise to keep its racing activities as clandestine as possible. But those activities had to take place. Given the fierce competition the upcoming Camaro would be facing from the Ford Mustang, the Chevy needed all the promotion it could get, so in August 1966, Piggins convinced Estes to develop a racing version of the Camaro for the new Trans-Am series.

Piggins faced a major engineering challenge in finding a suitable engine for the Camaro. The smallest V-8 available in the car—the 327-cubic-inch version—was too large to comply with SCCA's displacement limit of five liters, or roughly 305 cubic inches. Piggins answer was to put a crankshaft from the 283-cubic-inch small-block V-8 into a

The Z/28 featured an engine and suspension package developed for use on a racetrack.

modified 327-cubic-inch block, leading to a 302-cubic-inch engine with a bore of four inches and a stroke of three inches. This oversquare design meant the engine would have a lower piston speed at a given rpm, allowing the engine to have a higher redline.

A good suspension meant even more to the Camaro's racing success than did a fast engine. Piggins' team started with the best suspension available for the Camaro—the F41—and improved it. The racing version received stiffer rear springs, a thicker front anti-roll bar, and a radius rod similar to the one Pontiac was developing for its upcoming Firebird. Quicker steering gears and a stronger rear axle that allowed the use of disc brakes in the back as well as the front rounded out the suspension changes.

Piggins created the Z/28's 302-cubic-inch V-8 by using the crankshaft from a 283-cubic-inch V-8 and a modified block from the 327-cubic-inch engine.

This engine and suspension package would appear on a street car designed to homologate the Camaro for racing, and Chevrolet planned to build enough to qualify the car for SCCA's Trans-Am series. Cars intended for actual track use received further modifications, like heavy-duty spindles, axles, and shafts, along with special bushings and a 37-gallon fuel cell, a requirement if the car was to be competitive in the long-distance Trans-Am events.

Chevrolet's selection of a name wasn't quite as arbitrary as Carroll Shelby's selection of a name for his SCCA racer; Pete Estes didn't have Vince Piggins to pace off the distance between the Chevrolet commissary and the front receptionist's desk or anything of that sort. Chevrolet had designated the Trans-Am homologation package as "option Z-28." "We said, 'Damn, that's a good name,'" Pete Estes said, as quoted in Gary Witzenburg's book *Camaro!*, "so we pulled it out of the bag and put it on just the Camaro."

Chevrolet displayed the prototype Z/28 at Riverside, California, on November 26, 1966, and built the first production model on December 29 of that year. Drivers who knew how to wring out a peaky, high-revving engine liked the new car. *Car and Driver* magazine called the engine's horsepower rating of 290 "ridiculously conservative," comparing the acceleration of the Z/28 to a 426 Hemi. But most drivers preferred cars with big engines that produced big, tire-burning torque and Chevrolet sold just 602 Z/28s for the 1967 model year.

Pontiac called the top-of-the-line version of its 1969 Firebird the Trans Am, even though the car was not designed for or campaigned in SCCA Trans-Am racing. The 400-cubic-inch engine was far too big to slip under the upper displacement limit of the 302 cubic inches specified by the SCCA.

Cars like the Shelby GT350, Formula S Barracuda, and Z/28 Camaro held terrific potential as world-beating automobiles. Though rather crude in their original form (in a *Car and Driver* road test, an automotive journalist called the Shelby GT350 "a brand-new, clapped-out race car"), the Trans-Am homologation specials, with their lightweight engines and sporting suspensions, represented the most balanced performance cars built by the U.S. auto industry in the mid-1960s. But this was not an era defined by balance. It was an era defined by excess. Wretched excess. ■

CHAPTER 5

WRETCHED EXCESS

With the introduction of its redesigned B-body cars in 1968, Chrysler went from a non-player in the muscle car market to the dominant force.

Pontiac redesigned the GTO in 1966, giving the car the coke-bottle shape then in vogue.

Chrysler kicked off the era of wretched excess when it introduced the street Hemi as a regular production option for its redesigned 1966 B-body cars. Chrysler hadn't intended to create a street-racing legend when it unleashed the Hemi on an unsuspecting public, and it certainly hadn't intended to ignite a horsepower war between itself and its larger, better-funded rivals.

It simply planned to homologate the engine for NASCAR racing. Chrysler never intended to sell many Hemis for street use.

And it didn't. Chrysler sold more street Hemis than expected in 1966, but Hemi sales were eclipsed by the sales of B-body cars with other engines. Dodge sold a mere 468 Hemi-powered Chargers—1.2 percent of total Charger production—featured Hemi engines. The 325-horsepower 383-cubic-inch B-block, the next step down on the Chrysler engine hierarchy in 1966, made much more sense for the average driver. The 383 cost significantly less than the $1,000 price commanded by the Hemi, putting

it within the price range of the average buyer. Though it cost much less than the Hemi, the torquey 383 proved more satisfying in normal driving conditions. It had been designed for the stop-and-go driving encountered on city streets, and from 0-to-60 it was as quick as the expensive Hemi. Of course, at that point, the Hemi disappeared into the distance, leaving the 383 for dead, but the Hemi was never engineered for normal street use. It was designed to blast through the quarter-mile in as short a time as possible, or to run flat out for hours on end on superspeedways. Like so many racing homologation engines of the 1960s, the Hemi hadn't received an expensive redesign before seeing street use. It had merely been detuned, and driving one was like trying to modulate an on-off switch that unleashed a 500-horsepower explosion. To check the $1,000 Hemi box on the option sheet meant an owner wanted to do some serious drag racing, or else that he really, really, wanted to have bragging rights, because he certainly wasn't buying a car for practical transportation.

A Charger equipped with the 383 B-block engine, on the other hand, provided extremely practical transportation, as well as thrilling burn-outs when cruising Main Street on a Friday night, thanks to the engine's 425 ft-lb of torque.

The 1966 B-body cars sold well enough for Chrysler, though the model designed for the youth market—the Charger—failed to strike a chord with baby boomers. Compared to the 72,272 Chevelle SS 396s Chevrolet sold, the 96,946 GTOs Pontiac sold, and the

breathtaking 607,568 Mustangs Ford sold, the 37,344 Chargers sold indicated that Dodge's interpretation of a sporty car wasn't connecting with baby boomers.

The easiest way for Chrysler to make its B-body cars more appealing to younger buyers was to rely on the company's engineering expertise and expand the cars list of optional engines. In 1966 Chrysler had introduced a 350-horsepower 440-cubic-inch engine for its full-sized luxury cars, the Imperial and New Yorker. Because it gained its extra displacement in part through an increased stroke, Chrysler dubbed the engine family the RB series, "RB"

Though the street Hemi was offered as an option in passenger cars, it was really a race engine and not a good street option. Still, a small number of buyers ordered Hemis in their convertibles, as did the original buyer of this 1967 GTX.

Chrysler's 1966 and 1967 B-body muscle cars looked a bit old-fashioned compared to the competition from Ford and General Motors. Only Chrysler, however, offered a Hemi.

standing for "raised block." When used in the sporty B-body cars, the engine received a hot-rodding treatment consisting of special heads with 10 percent larger valves and stiffer valve springs, hotter camshafts, and a huge Carter AFB four-barrel carburetor. These tricks raised the horsepower rating to 375, the highest of any engine equipped with hydraulic lifters.

But peak horsepower was not what this engine was all about. It was about torque, lots and lots of tire-smoking torque. The engine, labeled "440 Magnum" when mounted in a Dodge and the "440 Super Commando" when mounted in a Plymouth, churned out a class-leading 480 ft-lb of torque.

In addition to a new engine for 1967, Chrysler offered a pair of new B-body models aimed squarely at the muscle car market: the Dodge Coronet R/T, which stood for "Road and Track," and the Plymouth GTX, which apparently stood for nothing in particular but sounded like a car that could kick a GTO's ass. When equipped with either the 440 or the 426 Hemi, it certainly had the stones to accomplish that task.

Chrysler offered the Hemi engine as an option in any of its 1966 B-body cars, even its bread-and-butter sedans like the Belvedere.

The new Mopars looked like they were ready to whup some ass too. Where the Charger had been a well-equipped personal-luxury car, these new B-body models were bare-knuckle street brawlers. The styling of these crisp, clean, purposeful cars has weathered the test of time much better than some of the cars' outrageous competitors, but in 1967 outrageous was in. Confused youngsters from across America and around the world were putting flowers in their hair and heading off to San Francisco, most of them without even knowing why they were going. The nation would soon experience the Summer of Love, a time in which young people would engage in acts so outrageous that their parents could not even imagine such despicable behavior a generation earlier. The year 1967 was not a good one for restraint, and Chrysler's B-bodies, with their restrained styling, suffered mightily. Charger sales fell to just 14,980 units, and sales of all three B-bodied muscle cars—the Charger, Coronet R/T, and GTX—totaled a mere 37,176 units, less than the Charger had sold alone the previous year. One bright spot for fans of Mopar muscle was that Hemi sales more than doubled. In 1967, 1,121 buyers found the testicular fortitude to equip their cars with the expensive Hemi engine.

The R/T version of the Charger came with a 440 Magnum as standard equipment. This car has an optional Hemi engine.

Plymouth offered three versions of the GTX in 1968: two-door post, two-door hardtop, and the convertible shown here.

It might not have been an ideal car for unwinding twisty roads, but a Hemi-equipped 1968 GTX convertible could transport a sun-worshipping drag racer down a quarter-mile strip of asphalt in short order.

ROLLING COKE BOTTLES

Up until this point, Chrysler had relied on its engineering prowess to compensate for its shortcomings in styling. As far as many younger buyers were concerned, Chrysler's B-bodies were only slightly more stylish than AMC Ramblers. This was a difficult fall from grace for a company that had become famous for its stylish cars a decade earlier.

That reputation had been built on the pen of Virgil Exner, who took over Chrysler's Advanced Studio in 1949. Exner saw the automotive world in graceful, fluid lines influenced by European coachbuilders like Ghia. Beginning with cars like the C-300, Exner designed some of the most elegant vehicles ever to roll out of Detroit. But trends change and Exner's design aesthetic didn't; by the early 1960s automotive design had moved in directions Exner wasn't willing to follow, and by the time his final designs appeared for the 1962 model year, his soft lines appeared antiquated.

One may wonder why an owner would equip a torque-monster engine like the Hemi with a four-speed transmission, but when discussing a Hemi-powered GTX convertible, it's often best not to ask "why?"

Chrysler spent most of the rest of the decade trying to catch up with the competition when it came to auto styling. When the Barracuda appeared in 1964, it represented a stylish alternative to the 1960 Ford Falcon and the 1962 Chevy II, but it couldn't compete with Ford's new Mustang. The Mustang's long hood and short rear deck forever changed the market's expectation for what a sporty four-seat coupe should look like, and the original Barracuda's miniature sedan proportions, even when disguised by a huge glass fastback, would never fit in with these changed expectations.

When the Charger hit the streets in 1966, it found itself in much the same situation as the Barracuda of a couple years earlier. Had the competition been the 1964 A-bodies from General Motors—the GTO, Chevelle, Skylark, and F-85 Cutlass—the Charger might have appeared more contemporary. Instead, Chrysler dropped the Charger into a market where it would have to compete with restyled A-bodies from General Motors. Instead of the slab-sided body panels of the original A-cars, the 1966 models featured what was referred to as "Coke-bottle" styling. Cars earned this nickname by having more rounded body panels with arcs over the wheel wells, making them resemble bottles of Coca-Cola laid on their sides. Chevrolet introduced this style to the American auto market with its 1963 Corvette and took it to its illogical extreme with the 1968 Corvette, though that car more closely resembled a prosthetic phallus than a Coke bottle. General Motors applied this style to its A-body cars for 1966 and experienced record sales.

Chrysler had applied Coke-bottle styling to its 1967 Barracuda, but it wasn't enough to make the newly handsome little car stand out among the long-hood-short-deck pony car competitors from General Motors and Ford. For 1968, Chrysler applied its

interpretation of the Coke-bottle styling treatment to its struggling B-body cars. The resulting machines, with their smooth lines, subtly rounded curves, and near-perfect proportions, were some of the most stunning automobiles of the classic muscle car era. The cars still looked as if they were itching for a fight, but they looked more like a brawny Hollywood movie star itching for a fight than a cauliflower-nosed ex-pugilist itching for a fight.

Engines remained unchanged for the most part—it was pretty hard to improve on the torque-monster 440 or the brutal Hemi. The 383-cubic-inch B-block received the improved heads off the 440 Magnum, bumping power output up to 335 horses. When mated to a four-speed transmission, B-bodies equipped with the new 383 Magnum provided an extremely entertaining ride.

Dodge introduced a restyled Charger and Coronet R/T for 1968, along with a new R/T rendition of the Charger. The Charger R/T package consisted primarily of the addition of a few cosmetic badges, though it did include one critically important piece of standard equipment: the 375-horsepower 440.

Plymouth added a companion model for the GTX, a raw street racer even more bare-bones than the R/T. This represented a move in the opposite direction from the trends muscle cars had been following throughout the decade. They had grown larger, heavier, more luxurious—in other words, flabbier. Plymouth thought there might be a market for a trimmed-down hot rod in the mold of the original GTO. They took the lightest, least-expensive version of the B-body chassis—the coupe—and stripped it of all frills like bucket seats and carpeting. They endowed the car with the heavy-duty suspension from Chrysler's police package and gave it the 335-horsepower version of the 383 as standard equipment. Best of all, they priced the car at $2,896, making it the performance bargain of the classic muscle car era.

Chrysler had had enough of restraint. In one of the most outrageous marketing moves of the period, Plymouth licensed the use of a popular Warner Brothers' cartoon character and named the car Road Runner. The hot rod Plymouth featured graphics of the cartoon bird as well as a dual-toned horn designed to ape the Road Runner's distinctive "meep-meep" voice. This was not a car for a shrinking violet who wanted restrained, inconspicuous transportation. If an owner wanted to abandon any semblance of restraint, he could order a 426 Hemi. When equipped with a Hemi, the lightweight Road Runner became the fastest regular production stock car of the 1960s.

The new models from Chrysler seemed perfect for the market, but there was no guaranteeing they would not suffer the same fate as earlier Chrysler attempts at reaching baby-boomers, especially since they dropped at the same time as a new intermediate from Ford and dramatically restyled A-bodies from General Motors.

The GTX was Plymouth's answer to the Dodge Charger—an upscale, well-equipped muscle car marketed to affluent buyers.

A 1970 convertible Coronet R/T Hemi is a study in contrasts, offering the relaxed, open-air feel of a convertible and the tense, brutal power of the 426-cubic-inch Hemi V-8.

Because the potent Hemi engine raised havoc with a flexible convertible chassis, few buyers combined the two. As a result, convertibles with Hemi engines are rare. Original examples are the most valuable cars on the market today.

BLUE OVAL MUSCLE

In 1968, Ford introduced its first new entrant aimed directly at the youth market since the Mustang: the Torino GT. The Torino was part of a plan to phase out the Fairlane nameplate. Pedestrian Torinos still carried Fairlane badges, but these were absent on the GT. The Torino was slightly larger than the Fairlane and featured fastback styling that resembled the 1966–1967 Charger. To many young customers, this represented dated styling, but Ford designers were more interested in aerodynamic efficiency than gaining market share, since the Torino would form the basis for the company's NASCAR racing efforts.

By this time, engineers had reached the upper limits of horsepower using normally aspirated pushrod V-8 technology, at least until perfecting advanced electrical controls and fuel injection technology. This would not happen for a few more years, so Ford had

By 1970, no self-respecting muscle car came without an outrageous hood scoop or two.

to resort to methods other than raw horsepower to attain a top-speed advantage over the competition. The most promising way to attain extra speed was to improve aerodynamic design. A small increase in aerodynamic efficiency increased top speed as much as a large increase in total horsepower output. The Torino may have featured styling that would not set the muscle car world on fire, but it worked on NASCAR's superspeedways. Driver David Pearson dominated the 1968 season in a Holman-Moody–prepared Torino GT, winning 16 races and finishing in the top five 36 times. The Torino's aerodynamic design had helped Ford finally break the Hemi's dominance of NASCAR's Grand National series.

Ford listed an optional big-block engine for the Torino GT, a hydraulic-valve version of the 427-cubic-inch FE-block engine that powered Pearson's car to victory, but there is no record of such a car actually being built. The top engine choice a regular customer could order for his or her Torino when the car debuted was the same 390 big-block engine found in the Mustang.

Pearson's 1968 result validated Ford's Total Performance concept. Throughout the 1960s, Total Performance had manifested itself in two distinct ways: performance cars for the street and performance engines for racing. In the mid-1960s, Ford laid most of its total street performance eggs in the Mustang's basket. Making the Mustang the focus of its efforts to market a car to baby boomers had been a wise

The Coronet R/T was originally conceived as a more affordable alternative to the luxurious Dodge Charger, but by 1970, it had grown as opulent and feature-laden as its upscale sibling.

A car like the Hemi-powered Coronet
R/T convertible might make little or no
sense as practical transportation, but
there is no denying the car's appeal.

The Charger lost its fastback with the 1968 redesign, but it retained a handsome (if aerodynamically awful) tunnel-like rear window.

choice for Ford. The company sold nearly 1.3 million Mustangs before Chevrolet even brought its pony car on the market.

When it came to total racing performance, Ford cast its seed across a broader furrow, competing in sports car, stock car, open wheel, and drag racing events. Ford Motor developed high-performance V-8 engines that often were the ones to beat on a racetrack. Its first race engine to attain dominance was the 427-cubic-inch NASCAR engine, a development of the 406 FE-block engine. Released in 1963, this engine used such exotic technology as cross-bolted main bearing caps, impact-extruded pistons, forged-steel exhaust valves with chrome stems, and transistorized electronic ignition. The drag racing version of this engine, which used a pair of four-barrel carburetors, developed 425 horsepower. When equipped

with a single four-barrel carb, as required by NASCAR's regulations, it generated 410 horsepower. Galaxies powered by the new Ford engine captured the top five spots at the Daytona 500 in 1963, and Ford went on to win the manufacturer's championship that year. Ford homologated the engine by building lightweight Galaxies equipped with the engine, but these were pure racecars with fiberglass hoods and fenders. They lacked the most basic accoutrements of a passenger car, like heaters and sound-deadening insulation.

While Ford dominated NASCAR's Grand National series in 1963, it had less success in NHRA drag racing. The problem was its car, the Galaxie. Even with all the drastic weight-saving measures taken with the lightweight models, the basic car was still too big and too heavy to be successful against the lighter competition from Chrysler. For 1964, Ford mounted the engine in its intermediate-sized Fairlane. With the use of fiberglass body panels, Ford got the weight down to a bit over 3,200 pounds. The resulting car, dubbed the Thunderbolt, was fast enough to bring home a couple of NHRA titles that year.

It seemed as if Ford could either succeed at drag racing or stock car racing, but not at both. In 1964, Ford lost the lead it had held in NASCAR racing the previous year, thanks

INSET: In 1968 Plymouth licensed a popular Warner Brothers cartoon character for the name of its budget-priced muscle car: the Road Runner.

The standard engine in the 1968 Road Runner was a version of the 383-cubic-inch, B-block wedge V-8 with freer-flowing heads. But, if a buyer was willing to spend the money, he could upgrade to potent Hemi power.

The Hemi could be put to good use in a two-door hardtop like this 1969 Road Runner, a car with a rigid enough chassis to twist the big engine's prodigious torque into the pavement.

to the introduction of Chrysler's new Hemi-powered cars, which handed Ford's Galaxies their asses on superspeedways around the country. Since Ford's "Performance" would be less than "Total" without NASCAR championships, the company pulled out all stops in an effort to build a motor to outpower the Hemi. The result became known as the "Cammer," thanks to the camshafts perched atop each cylinder head. This overhead-cam engine, with its massive eight-foot-long timing chain in front of the block spinning each cam, cranked out an estimated 600 horsepower. Its size, weight, and insane power output made the Cammer wholly unsuitable for use in a street-going production car, and as a result Ford was unable to homologate the engine to meet NASCAR's requirements for eligibility. In NHRA drag racing the engine was only eligible for the F/X class. For NASCAR racing, Ford went back to using a slightly redesigned 427, a version nicknamed the "side-oiler" because it featured oil passages machined into the sides of the engine block. In 1965 Carroll Shelby won an FIA manufacturers world championship in part on the strength of this engine.

Like Chrysler's 426 Hemi, the heavy, brutish, temperamental Ford 427 engine had not been engineered for street use and made a poor choice for daily driving. Still, Ford had to sell passenger cars equipped with the engine to make it legal for racing. Though it doesn't seem to have been mounted in any 1968 Torino GTs, versions of the 427 had occasionally appeared in passenger cars over the years. Most of these were full-sized vehicles like the Mercury Marauder, with one notable exception. In 1967 Ford sold a version of the intermediate Fairlane equipped with a version of the 427 FE-block engine. Such a car should have been the toast of the muscle car world, but in reality its existence barely registered among auto enthusiasts at the time. Part of the problem was that the Hemi had already become something of an urban legend. Its status was such that a select group of people would pay the steep purchase price

The Plymouth Road Runner was the right car at the right time and sales took everyone by surprise, especially the competition from General Motors and Ford.

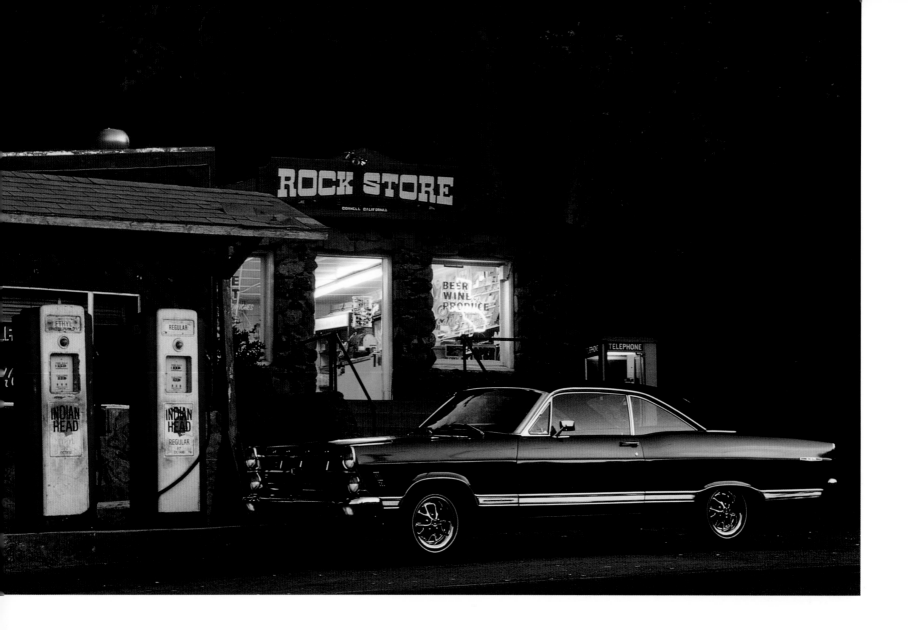

Fastback styling, a long wheelbase, and a 427 racing engine were the keys to the Fairlane's success on NASCAR ovals.

Engine badges announcing that a 427 racing engine lurked under the hood were the only outward clues distinguishing the XL500R from the pedestrian 1967 Ford Fairlanes sitting in church parking lots across America.

and tolerate the engine's foibles on the street just for the thrill of owning the mythical beast. Ford's 427 had no such cachet. The Fairlane's conservative styling didn't help its cause, either. Other than a small fender badge announcing the engine's 427-cubic-inch displacement, the Fairlane XL500 427R looked exactly like the car Grandma drove to church on Sunday morning. A car that could get lost in a church parking lot virtually disappeared when parked next to a sporty Mustang on a dealer's lot, monster motor or not.

In 1965 Ford developed a more streetable version of the FE-block engine for its large sedans. With milder tuning and hydraulic lifters, this 345-horsepowere engine was more tractable in the stop-and-go driving conditions encountered outside the confines of a racetrack. The engine lacked the durability of the side oiler when subjected to the extreme conditions of competition driving, but it made a good power plant for use in

Ford mounted less than 60 of its 427 racing engines in Fairlanes in 1967, building only the minimum number required to satisfy NASCAR's homologation rules.

Throughout the mid-1960s Ford focused its marketing efforts on selling the popular Mustang pony car. It wasn't until 1968 that Ford entered the traditional muscle car market with the Torino GT. Shown is a 1970 model.

a muscle car thanks to the 462 ft-lb of torque it generated. Though this engine displaced 426.9 cubic inches, Ford marketers, knowing that bigger numbers sounded better to customers' ears, dubbed the engine the 428 Cobra Jet. Midway through the 1968 model year, Ford made a version of this engine available in its Torino GT. When mounted in the Torino, the engine was rated at 335 horsepower, though this was a conservative estimate designed to prevent a buyer's insurance agent from totally freaking out.

BODACIOUS A-BODIES

The new Torino GT was just one of the cars Chrysler's new B-bodies were up against when vying for youth-market dollars in 1968. General Motors provided even more serious competition with its redesigned A-bodies. These cars applied pony car proportions—long hood, short rear deck, small passenger compartment—to GM's lineup of intermediate cars. Built on shorter wheelbases than previous A-body models, these cars began to encroach on the pony car market in size as well as style. Since the Mustang had grown in size for 1967, the distinction

between the pony car genre and the muscle car genre was starting to blur. The cars still featured curves over the wheel wells, but by blending the roofline into the rear deck in a semi-fastback style, designers moved away from a design that could reasonably be compared to a bottle of Coca-Cola.

Pontiac produced the most outrageously styled version of the new A-body platform. The 1968 GTO featured what GM's performance division called an "Endura" bumper, a body-colored, close-cell, urethane foam bumper bonded to a metal frame. The absence of a chrome bumper gave the GTO's front end a futuristic appearance unlike any car Detroit had ever produced.

Pontiac had introduced a revised V-8 engine for 1967 with better flowing cylinder heads. When mounted in the GTO, this engine displaced 400 cubic inches, the maximum capacity a nervous GM management would allow in its intermediate cars at the time.

The Torino GT got its muscle from a 428 Cobra Jet engine, conservatively rated at 335 horsepower.

The 1969 Ford Torino Talladega marked a shift away from emphasis on horsepower and toward aerodynamic efficiency as a means for attaining supremacy on NASCAR superspeedways.

These timid souls also put the kibosh on multiple carburetion in 1967, in an attempt to mollify a growing number of safety zealots hell-bent on saving hot rodders from themselves. This group, led by *Unsafe at Any Speed* author Ralph Nader, rattled the cages of GM corporate management. General Motors tried to find a compromise between Nader's safety nazis and the public's demand for more power. Pontiac's 400-cubic-inch engine was one example of such a compromise. While the triple-two-barrel carb setup was history, the increased displacement and freer-flowing heads meant that the high-output version of the new engine retained the 360-horsepower rating of its Tri-Power 389-cubic-inch predecessor.

Pontiac introduced an interesting option for the GTO in 1967: the Ram Air system. Pontiac supplied this system in the trunks of Ram Air–equipped GTOs and specified it for

use only in dry weather. This system consisted of a second ornament for the hood scoop, one that lacked the block-off plates of the standard scoop. This effectively turned the fake hood scoop into a real one. A driver could remove the standard plate with three speed screws and install the Ram Air system, though he or she was supposed to replace the standard plate in the event of any precipitation.

The redesigned 1966 Pontiac GTO was a mild refresher created by adding curvaceous bodywork to the existing 1965 chassis.

By 1967, the GTO's traditional sedan proportions were looking dated. Buyers wanted the look of the popular pony cars, the Mustangs, Camaros, and Firebirds.

INSET: In 1967, an eight-track tape deck was state-of-the-art in automotive audio systems.

When Pontiac introduced the restyled GTO for 1968, it included what it called the Ram Air II option. Like the original Ram Air, the breathing equipment Pontiac supplied came in the car's trunk. But the scoop inlets were the least important part of Ram Air II. Of more importance to a driver's right foot were new round-port cylinder heads with polished and tuliped valves, a wilder camshaft, and freer-flowing exhaust manifolds. In addition, Pontiac moved the air inlets up higher on the hood of the redesigned GTO, where they could scoop more air into the engine compartment. The result of all this fine tuning was that when equipped with Ram Air II, the 400-cubic-inch engine generated 366 horsepower.

The results paid off. *Motor Trend* magazine picked the GTO as its car of the year and sales rose to 87,684 units, up nearly 6,000 units over the previous year. More importantly for Pontiac, the division sold over 340,000 Tempest models, including the GTO, putting Pontiac second behind Chevrolet in the intermediate car market and ahead of every other brand.

BUICK'S BAROQUE MUSCLE

Rival GM divisions Oldsmobile and Buick were just bit players in the muscle car melodrama in the late 1960s. Buick especially struggled to connect to the youth market. The division's marketers resorted to outright deception in an attempt to siphon off some baby-boom dollars. Buick's marketing team wanted to cash in on Pontiac's strong GTO sales, and they knew that big numbers sold cars in a market obsessed with more of everything. Even though its 401-cubic-inch muscle car engine displaced more cubic inches than the Pontiac engine, the souped-up Pontiac mill produced more power

Buyers purchased 81,000 GTOs in 1967. Pontiac sold roughly the same number of Firebirds that year, but the 1967 Firebirds were only sold for a few months before the 1968 models debuted, indicating a higher demand for Pontiac's pony car than for its traditional muscle car.

than the 335-horsepower Buick. The one area where the Buick engine excelled was in torque production. The Buick engine pumped out an impressive 445 ft-lb of twisting force. To capitalize on that, Buick's marketing team named the engine the Wildcat 445.

This ruse did not help Buick's cause. Sales plummeted for the 1966 model year, falling 80 percent from 1965 levels. The original GM performance division desperately needed to create a car that the youth market would covet if it wanted to avoid getting a reputation as GM's Rambler division. Buick's rendition of the 1968 A-body had to stand apart from the crowd if it was to sell to baby boomers. The lines Buick's designers penned certainly made the car stand out among its A-body brethren. Rather than the smooth curves of the

GM redesigned its A-body muscle cars for 1968, giving them the same trendy, long-hood, short-deck proportions used in its pony cars. Shown here is a 1969 GTO.

With its sedan-like styling and small-block engine, the Buick GS-340 only triggered the buy impulse in 3,892 buyers in 1967. The baby-boom generation just didn't want small-block engines producing only 260 horsepower.

Oldsmobile's 4-4-2 looked a bit more contemporary than Buick's Gran Sport in 1967, but by that time it was clear even to GM's famously obtuse management that the company's A-body muscle cars needed a dramatic redesign if they were to remain competitive.

Oldsmobile's redesigned 4-4-2 featured exaggerated fender flares that complemented the new A-body's curvy shape perfectly. This 1969 example features Oldsmobile's W-30 package.

Because GM's corporate policies still forbade mounting engines larger than 400 cubic inches in intermediate cars, Oldsmobile went off the reservation to create the 455-cubic-inch Hurst/Olds cars. Hurst Performance built just less than 1,500 of these big-block monsters in 1968 and 1969.

other A-bodies, they split the sides of the car with an accent ridge that started at the top of the headlight, ran over the fender, then curved down toward the rear wheel well, giving the car a droopy-jowl look. The market responded as one would expect; while sales of the A-body muscle cars from other GM divisions rose for the 1968 model year, Gran Sport sales continued to flatline. The addition of a functional fresh-air induction system in 1969 wasn't enough to overcome the Gran Sport's frowning-octogenarian profile, and sales fell another 40 percent that year. With total Gran Sport sales of just 8,132 units in 1969, Buick's position in the youth market couldn't have been grimmer if division stylists had drilled portholes in the car's unfortunate front flanks.

HURST OLDS

For Oldsmobile, the stakes in the intermediate market were even higher than they had been for Buick, and the success of its new-for-1968 A-body was critically important to the division. While Oldsmobile's total sales fell in 1967 and the company slipped from fifth to sixth place in the marketplace, sales of the division's A-body cars had actually risen that year. Olds did not want to mess up the one car in its lineup that sold well.

Even though Oldsmobile sold large numbers of its rendition of the A-body, most of the nearly half-million F-85s the division moved in 1966 and 1967 went to elderly buyers. The Cutlass was the intermediate car of choice for the blue-haired crowd. Barely 10 percent of its F-85 customers purchased the sporty 4-4-2 version. Even at that early date the division's customer average age was getting dangerously high. Its cars just didn't connect with baby boomers. The 4-4-2 was a capable car with arguably the best suspension of any A-body variant, but its conservative styling meant that most young buyers didn't even notice the car existed.

George Hurst received 4-4-2 chassis from Oldsmobile and installed breathed-on 455-cubic-inch V-8s at his plant in Lansing, Michigan, along with nearly every luxury item in the Hurst Performance catalog.

Since Hurst Performance was famous for high-quality shifters, the Hurst/Olds' had to have the best equipment Hurst offered, in this case one of the company's Dual-Gate systems for GM's three-speed automatic.

Oldsmobile designers did a commendable job in making the 4-4-2 version of the 1968 Cutlass distinctive-looking, perhaps not as distinctive as Pontiac's GTO, but on par with Chevrolet's restyling effort and leaps and bounds ahead of Buick's sad Gran Sport. Performance equalled that of the muscle cars from competing GM divisions too, at least when the car was equipped with the W-30 package, which featured a 360-horsepower, 400-cubic-inch engine.

Three hundred and sixty horses were good, but by this time GM's A-bodies were starting to earn a reputation as underpowered. Compared to Chrysler's 440 Magnum and 426 Hemi, and Ford's soon-to-be-released 428 Cobra Jet, the 400-cubic-inch displacement dictated by corporate headquarters was starting to seem a bit puny. George Hurst, owner of Hurst Performance Products, sensed there might be an opportunity to capitalize on the squeamishness of GM management and approached Olds with a proposal to build some special editions of its 4-4-2. Hurst guessed—rightly—that Oldsmobile's desperation to reach the youth market might make his proposal an easy sell.

The plan was simple: do an end run around GM's corporate babysitters and build a muscle car with the biggest engine to date. Oldsmobile shipped Cutlasses without engines to Hurst's facilities in Lansing, Michigan. They also shipped Hurst their largest engines, the 455-cubic-inch big-blocks used in the division's luxury sedans. Hurst mildly hot-rodded the engines, bumping power to 390 horses and torque to 500 ft-lb.

In addition to power, the Hurst/Olds cars featured every luxury in the Oldsmobile catalog, and quite a few options unique to Hurst. It seemed to be exactly the kind of car the market wanted. Hurst sold cars as fast as he could build them, which, unfortunately for fans, was not very fast. His Lansing facility produced slightly less than 1,500 cars in 1968 and 1969. The baby boomers' reception of these Hurst/Olds proved that there was a market for a GM muscle car with a monster V-8 engine, a lesson GM management was not yet willing to learn.

THE STRANGE CASE OF THE TEN MISSING PONIES

Chevrolet fared much better than Buick and Olds with its redesigned 1968 A-body. Beginning with the ultra-low-volume Z16 package of 1965, Chevy had developed a reputation for high performance that translated into sold cars. When it restyled the Chevelle for 1966, it introduced a new model: the SS396. As the name implies, the 396-cubic-inch

version of the Mark IV big-block became the standard engine for the SS model. Chevrolet offered the 396 in three states of tune for 1966. The base engine for this car was the 325-horsepower L35, and an optional 360-horsepower L34 version, new for 1966, was available. The 375-horsepower L37 engine from the Z16 of 1965 didn't make the option list in 1966. The 1966 Chevelle SS396 received a stiffer suspension to cope with the added weight and power, and to help tame the A-bodied cars' tendency to understeer in corners.

In the spring of 1966 Chevrolet released another optional engine, the L78. With a bump in compression, solid lifters, and the big-valve cylinder heads off of the Corvette's 427-cubic-inch engine, the L78 generated 375 horsepower. A good selection of engines combined with the lowest base price of any of GM's A-bodied muscle cars helped Chevrolet sell 72,272 Chevelle SS396 models for 1966. Only 3,099 of those left the factory with the L78 engine.

George Hurst and Oldsmobile management understood that to compete in the muscle car market of the late 1960s, a car needed to have engines with more than 400 cubic inches, and Oldsmobile sold Hurst/Olds' as fast as Hurst could build them.

Like its corporate cousins, Chevrolet's Chevelle was ready for a complete redesign by 1967.

In a move that typified how truly out of touch GM's top management was with the car-buying public, the only major change to the SS396 for 1967 was a decrease in the horsepower rating for the optional L34 engine, the most popular power plant in the SS396 stable. The decreased rating doesn't appear to have been the result of any engineering changes. Rather, it seems to have been an attempt by GM's corporate management to throw Ralph Nader and his safety nazis a bone. In 1966, GM had changed the 10-pounds-per-cubic-inch rule to 10-pounds-per-horsepower. Instead of messing with the engine of one of its most

When Chevrolet introduced the 1968 Chevelle, it brought out one of the classic designs of the muscle car era.

Even from a dog's point of view of the 1968 Chevelle has appealing lines.

popular models, Chevrolet simply changed the horsepower rating of the L34 from 360 to 350, which, when mounted in the 3,500-pound Chevelle SS396, skirted under the corporate limit. The 375-horsepower L78 disappeared from the regular production option list entirely.

The effects this move would have on sales were obvious to anyone but the oblivious suits running General Motors—Chevelle SS396 sales decreased dramatically in 1967.

Fortunately for performance fans, GM's arbitrary new rules proved even more difficult to enforce than the old 10-pounds-per-cubic-inch rule. Zora Arkus-Duntov managed to continue mounting multiple carburetors on his Corvette sports car, and options like the L78, while not advertised as regular production options, continued to be available as unadvertised dealer-installed options. This loophole would open the door to all kinds of mayhem and madness in the final years of the decade by allowing clever Chevrolet dealers to mix and match parts, quietly encouraged by GM's merriest prankster Vince Piggins, to create the most outrageous muscle cars of the era.

In the face of decreasing sales, Chevrolet felt pressure to nail the design of its 1968 A-bodies. The basic shape of the new A-body had the right pony car proportions for the period. Somehow Buick managed to screw up the clean lines of the basic design, but division stylists had to work at it. Chevrolet kept it simple and its new A-body cars looked great. Engine options remained unchanged for 1968, though management relented and allowed the division to offer the L78 as a regular production option toward the end of the model year. This saved the engine from the clandestine gulag of the dealer installation program, where only well-connected gearheads knew how to find it.

Though Pontiac fancied itself an up-market alternative to Chevrolet, its designers were hard-pressed to create a more opulent interior than that found in a well-equipped Chevelle.

The base engine in the 1968 Chevelle SS396 was the 325-horsepower version of the Mark IV 396. While this made the standard SS396 a fast car, it was a bit underpowered compared to the engines offered by the competition, especially from Chrysler.

Factors other than the lack of a truly big big-block V-8 hindered sales of muscle cars as the 1960s wound down, such as the increasing number of young men being sent to Vietnam each year.

In 1968 and 1969 the Chevelle featured a distinctive rear quarter window that slanted backward as it rose toward the roofline. In 1970 this window was replaced by a more conventional piece.

The Chevelle sold in smaller quantities than expected, due in part to intense competition. Chevrolet itself produced a competitor that cannibalized Chevelle sales: the Nova SS.

The 1968 redesign of the Chevelle was generally well received, and the SS396 version of the car made a solid base for hot-rodders wanting to build serious street fighters, but sales once again declined. Part of the sales decline can be attributed to the failure of General Motors management to fully engage in the horsepower wars raging in Detroit at the time, but another reason for the decline was occurring half a planet away, in the jungles of Vietnam.

Throughout the mid-1960s the U.S. military had been sending troops to Vietnam in increasing numbers. By the summer of 1965 more than 125,000 U.S. troops were stationed in the far-off little country in Southeast Asia. A year later that number had risen to nearly half a million. In January 1968 the North Vietnamese army began what became known as the Tet Offensive, the bloodiest battle of the entire Vietnam war. To replenish troop strength, the U.S. army began to increase the number of young males it conscripted into military service. The bulk of these conscripts were young blue-collar males from the very demographic group that bought muscle cars. As the war droned on, these potential muscle car customers were being killed in alarming numbers. More than 58,000 U.S. soldiers perished in the conflict. Shipping a half-million potential Chevelle SS396 customers to the other side of the world did not make Chevrolet's job of selling muscle cars any easier.

Still another factor in declining Chevelle SS396 sales was an increasingly crowded muscle car market. Ford offered the Torino GT along with a bewildering array of Mustangs. The other General Motors divisions all had their A-body muscle cars, and Pontiac had its hot-selling Firebird. In addition to its own F-body Camaro, the Chevelle had to contend with another Chevrolet product cannibalizing SS396 sales: a Chevy II Nova SS, redesigned for 1968.

Chevrolet based the new car on the Camaro platform, which made sense since the Camaro had been based on the previous Chevy II platform. The Nova SS looked a bit like a swollen Camaro, thanks to its enlarged passenger compartment, but it was a handsome, well-proportioned car none-the-less. All sense of proportion went out the window, however, if a buyer opted for the newly available 375-horse L78 engine. This motor turned the lightweight Nova into a smoking-fast muscle car that could eat GTOs for breakfast. Chevy II sales nearly doubled for 1968, an increase that came in part at the expense of the Chevelle.

FLEXING MOPAR MUSCLE

One source of competition in the 1968 muscle car market came from an unexpected direction: Mopar's newly energized B-body lineup. Mopar had long had a corner on the "muscle" part with its Hemi and wedge engines, but the stodgy styling of the cars themselves made them the choice of foaming speed freaks hell-bent on tearing up quarter-mile drag strips. The average baby boomer opted for something more stylish from Ford or General Motors. Its restyled-for-1968 B-body lineup failed to adopt trendy pony car proportions, but apparently that was just fine by baby boomers. Sales of the redesigned 1968 Charger exploded to nearly 100,000 units, topping the sales of Pontiac's car of the year, the GTO. Nearly 75,000 Charger buyers chose the standard 383-equipped car, and the bulk of the rest selected the 440-equipped R/T. Chrysler's other B-bodied muscle cars sold well, too, especially the barebones Road Runner. Plymouth moved 44,595 examples of their outrageous cartoon cars for 1968.

Encouraged by the success of the Road Runner, Dodge developed its own cartoon car midway through the 1968 sales year. Rather than license an existing cartoon character, Dodge created its own: the Super Bee. Like the Road Runner, the Super Bee was a stripped-down version of Dodge's B-body coupe—the Coronet—that came with a standard 383 Magnum engine and a four-speed transmission. And like the Road Runner, the Super Bee could be ordered with an optional 426 Hemi engine. Sales of the Super Bee helped push total sales of B-body muscle cars to 173,872 units. This was on top of the sales of pedestrian B-body Coronets, Belvederes, and Satellites, which totaled 582,315 units. The year 1968 was a very good one for Chrysler Corporation.

Perhaps the most remarkable statistic for all of 1968, at least regarding automobile sales, was the number of buyers selecting Chrysler's optional Hemi engine. Chrysler sold 2,276 Hemi-powered B-bodies in 1968, an all-time record. Almost half of those elephant engines ended up in the lightweight Road Runner. Apparently a lot of people were willing to pay a steep entrance fee and undertake the challenges associated with owning and maintaining a street Hemi in return for the privilege of driving the baddest-assed car on the road.

For 1969, Chrysler chose not to mess with a good thing and the lineup returned largely unchanged, although the Super Bee and Road Runner models received an engine option that was outrageous even by 1969 standards: the A12 Six-Pack. This was a version of the high-performance 440-cubic-inch engine with a trio of Holley two-barrel carburetors mounted atop its specially designed, Edelbrock-built, aluminum intake manifold. In stock form this engine cranked out 390 horsepower. To cope with the added 15 horsepower, the engine received beefier valvetrain components. Although expensive at $462.80, a Six-Pack-equipped Mopar cartoon car provided its owner with more easily accessible power than any other muscle car on the market, at least when properly tuned. As these cars aged it became challenging to keep the three Holleys running in perfect unison, and they did not respond well to the meddling of ham-fisted would-be backyard mechanics.

In an attempt to capitalize on the success of Plymouth's wildly popular Road Runner, Dodge introduced its own cartoon muscle car: the Super Bee.

MEET THE NEW BOSS

In late 1967, GM's directors passed over Semon E. "Bunkie" Knudsen, for the position of corporation president. When Henry Ford II learned this top GM executive was available, he recommended his board promote Ford corporation president, Arjay Miller, to vice chairman, opening a key spot for Knudsen. Bunkie, a product-oriented and innovative car-enthusiast, had encouraged the creation of the Camaro and its Trans-Am-race-series-inspired Z/28 while at GM. He had vigorously pushed Pontiac division's GTO and other John DeLorean–directed inspirations. Now Knudsen, who knew GM's plans for a few years ahead, unleashed the furies of hell on his former employer.

On February 6, 1968, Knudsen arrived at Ford World Headquarters and moved into the president's office there. To him, this was the chance to get as much good-looking, fine-handling Ford horsepower into the marketplace as possible, and to do it fast. He quickly learned that the corporation already had several projects ready that would race toward that goal. Of particular interest to the muscle-car-friendly Knudsen was the mating of the 428 Cobra Jet engine with the intermediate Torino GT and the Mustang pony car.

The Super Bee was originally intended to be a lower-cost alternative to the Charger, but as with the Road Runner and Coronet R/T, most buyers equipped their cars with nearly every option in Dodge's catalog. This model even has a Hemi.

Rather than licensing a cartoon character from a movie studio as Plymouth had done with the Road Runner, Dodge invented its own cartoon character, the Super Bee, a play on the car's B-body heritage.

Knudsen wasted no time, and within months of his arrival Ford division had the 428 Cobra Jet Mustang ready for introduction as a mid-year 1968 model. As a rather costly ($434) option, the 428's 335-horsepower rating disappointed some enthusiasts. However, buyers and drivers quickly learned how conservative this number was. *Hot Rod* magazine tested a 428CJ in a Mustang fastback and achieved 0 to 60 miles per hour in 5.9 seconds, and standing start quarter-mile runs at 106.6 miles per hour in 13.56 seconds. From the factory, the engine developed more than 400 actual horsepower, yet its deceptive rating granted it more competitive placement in lower classes for NHRA and AHRA (American Hot Rod Association) amateur and professional events.

Ford offered it only in the GT package, which included a Ram-Air functional cold-air induction hood scoop (the CJ-R) and power front disc brakes. Buyers could order the car with either an automatic three-speed transmission or a four-speed manual. While Ford assembled 654 notchbacks, it produced 2,253 fastbacks, and a handful of convertibles emerged as well. To keep it on the road, Goodyear introduced its wider F70 poly-glass tires for the Cobra Jet.

A stealth version of the Cobra Jet Mustang arrived in 1969, and Ford offered it only through 1970. Known as the Super Cobra Jet, buyers had to understand the dealer order forms to find it hidden among option codes. While it was never specifically labeled the SCJ, buyers received it when they ordered the Drag Pack Axle option. The base hardtop

A 440 equipped with the A12 Six Pack option—conservatively rated at 390 horsepower—could give the vaunted Hemi a run for its money at the drag strip and made a much better street engine.

The 1968 Shelby GT500KR turned in quarter-mile times of under 15 seconds.

or SportsRoof retailed for $2,618 in 1969, and adding the normal Ram Air 428 Cobra Jet was a $421 option. After selecting the transmission and whatever other items the buyer desired, spending that last $155 replaced the CJ with the SCJ and added a 3.91:1 Traction-Lok rear end. The primary functional improvements of the Super Cobra Jet engine over the regular 428 Cobra Jet were more durable crankshafts, rods, pistons, along with a harmonic balancer, all designed to help the engine better withstand the higher RPM requirements of drag racing. If absolute performance with no road comfort compromise was the goal, Ford's knowledgeable dealers suggested spending yet another $52 for a 4.30:1 Detroit "Locker" differential and rear axle.

In 1969, Ford offered a pair of Mustangs that carried the nickname Larry Shinoda, a designer Knudsen had brought with him from General Motors, used for Knudsen: "Boss." The first car, the Boss 302, was a purposeful racer designed to win Trans-Am

The 1967 Shelbys were the last ones built at the Shelby's Los Angeles International Airport shops.

Beginning mid-1968 Ford offered the 428 Cobra Jet engine in Mustang GS. Previously, the engine had been available only in the Shelby Mustangs.

Ford offered the 428 Cobra Jet only in the GT models. Savvy buyers who understood Ford's option list could order an even more potent Super Cobra Jet, which also featured a functional ram-air hood scoop.

INSET: Though Ford rated the 428 Cobra Jet at just 335 horsepower, the Mustang's quarter-mile times of under 14 seconds proved that rating to be pessimistic. Real output was probably closer to 400 horsepower.

championships. The second, the Boss 429, was a balls-to-the-wall muscle car designed to homologate Ford's new NASCAR engine.

With many engine parts from Ford's GT40 race car installed in the 302 racing blocks, the factory racing version of the Boss 302 developed 500 reliable horsepower at an astonishing 9,000 rpm. Production versions put out 290 horsepower at 5,800 rpm, but even those gained 20 horsepower if a driver dared rev the engine to 7,000 rpm. The street 302 engine also adopted many of the technologies Ford engineering had invented and proven in the first 289-based engines for the GT40s as well.

As much as engines played a roll in the success of the Boss 302, so did its handling. Knudsen dictated, "'Make it absolutely the best handling street car available on the American market!'" according to author Donald Farr in *Mustang Boss 302: Ford's Trans-Am Pony Car*.

Ford's desire for superiority in NASCAR sparked the idea for the Boss 429. While Ford's 427-cubic-inch engines had been doing well enough in NASCAR's Grand National series, much of that success was attributable to aerodynamic efficiency. The engine itself was getting a bit long-in-tooth and engineering envisioned the 429 as its successor.

Ford's 429 was a semi-hemi, a design sometimes called a "crescent" head because the flat areas around the valve seats are crescent shaped. NASCAR required minimum production numbers of any engine to qualify it for racing, so Ford offered the 429 in the Boss, beginning in 1969.

Ford assembled the first 279 of the Boss 429 street engines with hydraulic lifters and cams. Sometime in mid-1969 Ford had revised the engine to use a mechanical cam. Rated conservatively at 375 horsepower, these Boss engines were assembled in Ford's Lima, Ohio, engine facility. However, once engines were completed, car assembly became quite complex. Engines left Lima and went to Kar Kraft, a kind of official-unofficial Ford fabrication and racing shop that had first developed the Boss 302 and 429 engines for racing. Everything was sent to the Kar Kraft facility in Brighton, Michigan. The engines came in from Ohio and completed cars arrived from Ford's River Rouge plant.

Complication arose because Rouge refused to build cars without engines, even though Kar Kraft didn't want the 428s the Rouge plant assembled. To keep peace, Kar Kraft accepted the Boss 429s off the assembly line with 428CJ engines installed, along with all the modifications necessary for the CJ package to become the big Bosses. Kar Kraft's people drove the cars onto transporters, trucked them to Brighton, and removed their engines, which were placed in storage. The Kar Kraft crews did some suspension modifications, installed the 429 engines and oil coolers, relocated the batteries to the trunk, and fitted the huge, front hood scoops, racing mirrors, and decals. Then Kar Kraft returned the completed Boss 429s to the Rouge plant for distribution.

The Trans-Am racing homologation special Boss 302 was designed to be "the best-handling car on the American market."

The Boss 429 was not designed to be the best-handling car in its class. It was designed to homologate be Ford's new NASCAR racing engine.

Ford made the Boss 429 for just two years. The white car on the left is a 1969 model and the blue car on the right is a 1970.

The heart of the Boss 429 was its engine, designed to beat Chrysler on NASCAR's super speedways. This advanced engine, with its thin-wall castings and semi-hemispherical heads, had a ludicrously low horsepower rating of 375.

Ford and Kar Kraft produced 859 of the Boss 429s in 1969, but production only reached 499 in 1970. By comparison, the Boss 302 sold 1,934 in 1969. Magazine reviewers loved the performance, handling, and balance of the 302 version. Production jumped to 6,318 in 1970. The Boss 302 was a $676 option in 1969, while the 429-ci engine added $1,208 to the sticker. In 1970, Ford product planners made the Boss 302 a separate package, pricing it at $3,720 (compared to the $2,771 base price for a "SportsRoof," Ford's 1969 and 1970 designation for its 2+2 fastback body style). The 429 remained an option and its price went unchanged.

The stockpile of unused, unwanted 428CJ engines continued to grow at Kar Kraft until, according to Anthony Young in his *Ford Hi-Po V-8 Muscle Cars*, the Rouge plant nearly ran out of Cobra Jet engines. Kar Kraft saved the day by selling them back truck loads.

Of the big three U.S. automakers, only General Motors hadn't made the leap to wretched excess when it came to engine displacement. Chrysler's muscle cars, led by the Hemis, had already attained legendary status, and Ford had redeemed its early aversion to high performance by producing cars like the Torino GT and the Boss 429. Meanwhile, General Motors continued to operate under rules designed to enforce its corporate notions of the public good. The baby boom generation had rejected such rules when they were put forth by their parents, law-enforcement agencies, and political leaders; they certainly weren't about to accept such intrusions from a car manufacturer. Auto enthusiasts joked that GM stood for "General Mothers," and viewed the company's attitude as unwanted nagging. These buyers might have had to tolerate such nagging from their mothers, but they didn't have to take it from a multinational corporation. They could simply buy their cars from other manufacturers, and that's exactly what hundreds of thousands of them did. ∎

Kar Kraft, the firm that installed the Boss 429 engines in the Mustang chassis, had to perform major underhood surgery to make the big NASCAR engines fit between the Mustang's front wheels.

Chrysler didn't develop a serious contender for the pony car market until its E-body models—the Plymouth 'Cuda and Dodge Challenger—introduced for the 1970 model year.

The arrow on the hood of the 1969 AMC Hurst SC/Rambler provided direction for the airflow, should the airflow become confused.

In the late 1960s it seemed everyone was jumping on the cubic-inch bandwagon except General Motors. General Motors' timidity about building muscle cars with excessive muscle meant that Chevrolet never officially supplied its 427-cubic-inch Mark IV engine as a regular production option in a traditional muscle car—those would have to make do with the 396-cubic-inch rendition of the engine.

But the Bowtie Division did develop the 427-cubic-inch power plant for use in full-sized production cars and trucks, and also for the Corvette sports car, providing the fiberglass two-seater with plenty of muscle.

Chevrolet had already done the hard work of engineering a street engine from its Mark II racing motor. This development took place when the division engineered the Mark IV version of the 396-cubic-inch big-block. The main difference between the 396 and the 427 used in passenger cars and trucks was a bigger bore for the cylinders on the 427. In 1966, Chevrolet made the 427-cubic-inch Mark IV available in two forms: the 390-horsepower

L36 pedestrian version and the 425-horsepower L72. The L72 version featured forged aluminum pistons, forged crankshaft journals, and four-bolt main bearing caps. Mechanical lifters meant that the owner would have to deal with valve-lash adjustments. Chevrolet only offered the L72 in the Corvette for one year.

The L72 disappeared from Chevy's engine stable in 1967 (it would reappear as an option for the Impala SS in 1968 and 1969), but the Corvette got a selection of optional 427s that provided even more horsepower. The L68, a version with hydraulic lifters and a trio of Holley carburetors, produced 400 horsepower. The L71 was essentially the 1966 L72 with the triple-carb setup from the L68. For $368.65 (on top of the L71's price tag of $437.10, for a total cost of $805.75) a Corvette buyer could order regular production option L89 and get a pair of optional aluminum cylinder heads attached to his or her L71 engine. That engine only weighed 55 pounds more than a 327. But the most radical version of the 427 Chevy offered Corvette buyers in 1967 was the L88. It wasn't listed in the standard Corvette brochure, but the L88 was a regular production option in 1967.

In the mid-1960s, Chevrolet offered the 427 V-8 in its full-sized models, such as this 1966 Impala SS.

Chevrolet sold only 20 Corvettes equipped with the L88 in 1967, 80 in 1968, and 116 in 1969. Those 216 cars have achieved mythological status, especially the 20 cars made in 1967.

The L88 represented the crowning achievement of Zora Arkus-Duntov, the father of the Corvette, and his engineering team. By 1966 the team had developed a number of exotic big-block V-8 engines, but none that ever saw production. These included a 660-horsepower 427 that used a chain-driven overhead cam, much like Ford's Cammer, and a pushrod 427 hemi that generated 628 horsepower. The L88 grew out of this development program. This engine could be described as an L71 with standard aluminum heads, but the L88 was much more than that. It was strengthened for racing use wherever needed, and wherever possible it used weight-saving aluminum parts. Since this engine was intended for racing use instead of street driving, buyers who selected it could not get air conditioning, power steering, power windows, radios, or even heaters in the 1967 cars. Chevrolet rated the L88 at 430 horsepower at 5,200 rpm, but if a driver had the nerve to explore the upper ranges of the tachometer, it produced much more. Dyno checks had the engine at over 560 horsepower at the rear wheels. The Corvette had been designed as America's sports car, but with the addition of engines like the L88, it also served as a hyper-performance muscle car.

Though the full-sized 1966 Impala SS was too large to be considered a true muscle car, when equipped with Chevrolet's 427-cubic-inch engine it had plenty of muscle.

INSET: Chevrolet's SS package defined the interior of a sporty car in the mid-1960s—complete gauges, floor-mounted shifter, bucket seats.

Though General Motors prohibited Chevrolet from mounting its 427-cubic-inch V-8 in intermediate-sized muscle cars, it allowed the Bowtie division to install it in the Corvette sports car.

The ultimate expression of the 427-cubic-inch big-block Mark IV engine—and the most exotic pushrod V-8 engine ever produced by an American auto manufacturer—was the ZL-1, which was essentially an all-aluminum L88. The Chaparral racing organization originally developed the aluminum version of the Mark IV for use in a Can-Am racing chassis. Chaparral manufactured and built a dry-sump big-block based on the Mark IV design. This engine used aluminum heads with an aluminum block and featured iron cylinder liners. Chevrolet decided to develop a version of the Chaparral motor as a production racing engine, a task that fell to Arkus-Duntov. It took much detail engineering to craft a 427-cubic-inch engine out of mostly aluminum, and the engine wasn't ready for production until the 1969 model year. Chevrolet rated the engine at the same 430 horsepower as the L88, but every engine built produced well over 500 horsepower on the dyno.

The ZL-1 was one of the most technologically advanced engines produced in the 1960s. Except for the forged-steel crankshaft, connecting rods, and camshaft, almost every part of the engine was made of aluminum, including the 12.25:1 compression pistons and cylinder heads. The entire engine weighed about the same as one of Chevrolet's small-block V-8s. It was easily the most exclusive engine ever offered by an American auto manufacturer. The only car ever to receive the ZL-1 engine as a regular production option was the 1969 Corvette, and only three buyers checked the ZL-1 option box when ordering cars that year. This was not a surprising number, given that the $4,718.35 engine roughly doubled the price of the already-expensive Corvette. In all, Chevrolet built a total of 154 ZL-1 engines, 82 of which went to the parts departments of Chverolet dealerships.

COPO

General Motor's reluctance to provide its customers with the big-cube engines they demanded frustrated many Chevy fans, but where most saw obstacles others saw opportunities. Chevrolet had the stylish Super Sports: the Camaros, Novas, and Chevelles. And the Bowtie division possessed the engines, the Mark IV family of 427-inchers ranging from the pedestrian L36 to the insane ZL-1. It also had a little known system for combining the two: the Central Office Production Order program (COPO). This was a program that provided equipment not deemed useful for cars sold to the general public. Usually this took the form of special paint schemes for fleet vehicles and heavy-duty suspension parts and durable interior fabrics for taxicabs, but it also included high-performance parts for police use. This program provided an ideal means through which Chevrolet's renegade engineers could circumvent the corporate ban on racing and supply speed equipment to racers.

Vince Piggins made good use of the COPO program. Essentially, once Piggins and his cadre of engineers headed up by Gin Huffstater created some wild and wonderful prototype, Piggins worked the phones. He called dealers around North America, usually one in each major metropolitan area. He knew the owners already had high-performance customers with deep pockets. Piggins told each dealer about the new car or a new engine, and asked them how many they would take.

Piggins and other renegades within Chevrolet plotted ways to use this program to build the image of Chevy cars like the Camaro. Sales of the division's pony car had been strong, but Ford still sold more Mustangs than Chevrolet sold Camaros. Building a credible Camaro counterpart to the Boss 429 Mustang would have helped remake the Camaro's image, but GM management had yet to relent on its policies concerning horsepower-to-weight ratios.

Buyers who knew about Chevrolet's Central Office Production Order (COPO) program could circumvent General Motors' corporate ban on large-displacement engines in intermediate cars and equip their Chevelles with the company's big 427-cubic-inch V-8.

By exploiting the COPO program, buyers could even equip Camaros with the mighty 427.

Available only through Chevrolet's clandestine COPO program, the ZL-1 Camaro was designed to dominate the NHRA's Super Stock C and D classes, but the NHRA ruled the car ineligible for Super Stock racing, forcing it to compete in the F/X class, where it raced against all-out funny cars.

The all-aluminum, 427-cubic-inch ZL-1 is perhaps the most exotic motor of the classic muscle car era. Every one of the 154 engines that left Chevrolet's production line produced well over 500 horsepower on the dyno.

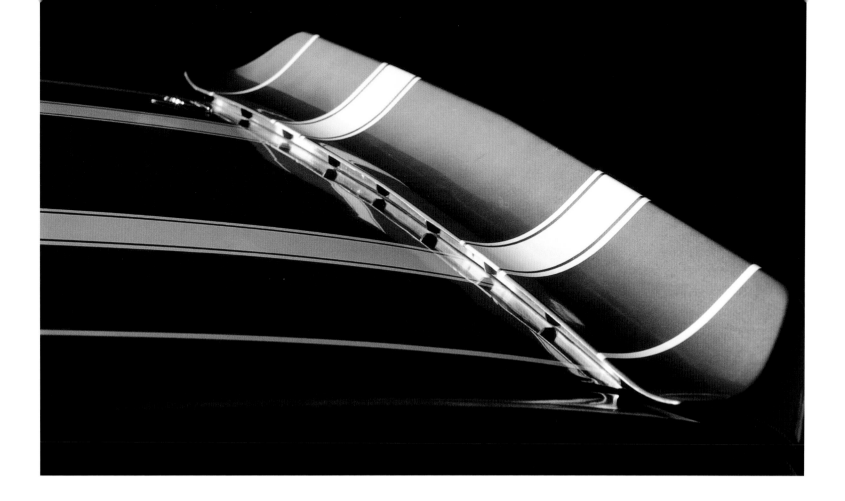

Installing the mighty ZL-1 engine in the Camaro would make it a Mustang stomper, but there was no way corporate brass would allow such a reprehensible act. Not only would it make Ralph Nader and his cronies apoplectic; it would not result in a very good street car. The engine had never been developed for street use and lacked such amenities as a choke. It had never been designed to use with a restrictive street exhaust system and the open-plenum manifold meant it would be all but undrivable on the street.

Mounting a ZL-1 engine in the lightweight Camaro body presented problems, but the idea was just too cool not to try it. The engine was given COPO code 9560 for Camaro use and offered through Piggins' clandestine program. If someone was brave enough or foolhardy enough to plunk down an extra $4,160 over the base price of the Camaro and request COPO option 9560, he received a ZL-1 engine with a Z/28 body wrapped around it, including the Z/28's racing suspension but without the Z/28 stripes. The cars featured street mufflers, which robbed the awe-inspiring engine of a bit of its thunder, but not enough to tame it. Even with its restrictive exhaust system, the car still possessed enough snort to make a trip to the grocery store a genuinely terrifying experience. Chevrolet hoped the high price of the ZL-1 engine would be enough to keep people from buying the car for anything but racing use.

The COPO program was designed to provide pedestrian equipment, such as durable vinyl for taxicab seats, but Chevy's racing czar Vince Piggins figured out how to use it to create some of the wildest muscle cars of all time, like this Camaro equipped with a ZL-1 racing engine.

Some Chevrolet dealers, like Don Yenko, used the COPO program to install monster motors in cars like the Camaro and Chevelle, creating more-muscular muscle cars.

INSET: "YENKO TUNED" meant that this 427-cubic-inch big-block generated 450 horsepower and 460 ft-lbs of torque. When powering a 3,500-pound Camaro, a Yenko-tuned 427 taught a high-speed lesson in physics.

Because General Motors had a policy limiting performance cars to 400-cubic-inch engines during the 1960s, the enterprising Don Yenko built his own big-inch Chevrolet muscle cars, like this 427 Camaro.

Chevrolet produced 69 of these outlandish cars, none of which made their mark at the drag strip. Although intended for racing use, ZL-1 Camaros were not very successful in NHRA racing. It wasn't because the cars were slow; a well-tuned ZL-1 Camaro could easily break into the 10-second bracket. The problem was the competition. Chevrolet rated ZL-1 horsepower at a ridiculously low 425 ponies so it could compete in Super Stock C and D classes, but the sanctioning bodies saw through the division's cheap ploy and classified it as a modified, where it would have to run against purpose-built race cars. By this time the F/X class had morphed into the funny-car classes and the 10-second ZL-1 Camaro found itself racing against all-out dragsters running through the quarter-mile traps in the 7-second bracket.

DEALER SPECIALS

Vince Piggins' group of resourceful Chevrolet dealers discovered the hidden secrets of the COPO program and exploited it to produce the cars General Motors should have built in the first place. Don Yenko typified this breed. Yenko owned Yenko Chevrolet, a Chevy dealership in Cannonsburg, Pennsylvania, just outside of Pittsburgh. He was also

Yenko cars like this Camaro have achieved the same rarified status as convertibles with Hemis in today's collector market.

When Yenko exploited the COPO program to install 427-cubic-inch engines in cars like this Chevelle, he built the cars Chevrolet should have been offering in the first place.

a life-long hot rodder and had achieved some success as a drag racer. In 1967, Yenko removed the engines from 54 SS350 Camaros and replaced them with the L72 version of Chevy's 427-cubic-inch engines. Those sold well so in 1968 he performed the same transplant on another 64 Camaro SS396s. Again, these cars sold well, but transplanting the engine required a lot of work and expense. Plus there was the issue of what to do with the leftover stock engines. In 1969, Yenko approached Chevrolet about forming a partnership for building 427-cubic-inch Camaros and Chevelles and selling them around the country. He convinced Chevrolet that he could sell 500 cars, enough to earn both Yenko and Chevrolet a profit.

Having seen the success Oldsmobile had with the Hurst/Olds, Chevrolet took Yenko up on his offer. Yenko souped up L72 versions of the 427 to produce 450 horsepower and mounted these engines in most of the Yenko Camaros and Chevelles he produced. He also built a few 427-powered Yenko Novas in 1969, but he felt these cars were unbalanced, and in 1970 he produced a Yenko Nova, called the Deuce, which featured the 350-cubic-inch LT-1 engine from the Corvette.

After an initial run of fewer than 40 cars, Yenko quit building the 427 Yenko Nova, deciding the engine was too powerful for the Nova platform. Yenko called the combination of a 427-cubic-inch V-8 and a 1969 Nova "lethal.".

Yenko and other dealers like Baldwin Chevrolet in New York, Nickey in Chicago, Berger in Michigan, Fred Gibb in Illinois, and Dana in California, filled a market need that General Motors was unwilling to fill. In doing so, they were following a historical precedent set by Jim Wangers a decade earlier. In 1959, Wangers had developed a partnership with Royal Pontiac in Royal Oak Michigan. This relationship led to Wangers' 1960 NHRA national championship in the Stock Eliminator class, and it led to a line of cars souped up at the Royal dealership. Called Royal Bobcats, these provided a test bed for developmental parts through the early years of the muscle car movement, and Royal Pontiac had prepared the ringer car Wangers used in the famous *Car and Driver* GTO versus GTO test. But the day of the dealer-prepped special was rapidly coming to a close, since General Motors was soon to relent and give its muscle cars some real muscle.

THE RAMBLER'S LAST RIDE

If American Motors Corporation was the redheaded stepchild of the U.S. auto industry, then the Rambler was AMC's Faulknerian idiot man-child. The AMX had drawn the company some much needed attention in the press, as had its Trans-Am racing effort, which culminated in national championships in 1971 and 1972. All this hadn't translated into the massive Javelin sales AMC hoped for, however. Meanwhile, the Rambler droned on in its monotone fashion, babbling non sequiturs about fuel economy to a world that wanted to hear about nothing but performance. By 1969, AMC had pulled the feeding tube from the Rambler's brain-dead carcass and the nameplate was in the process of wasting away.

Some elements within the company secretly fought for the Rambler's right to live. Deep within the corporate closets of American Motors lurked a small contingent of fetishists who harbored a love for the Rambler. These folks believed that AMC was making a mistake by killing the Rambler nameplate, and they plotted for its survival. Keeping the Rambler name alive was not an acceptable orientation to have as far as AMC's corporate hierarchy was concerned, and the company's Rambler cowboys had to go outside corporate halls to practice their love that dare not speak its name.

George Hurst of Hurst/Olds fame offered these corporate deviants sanctuary. Hurst agreed to take stripped-down Ramblers, strengthen their chassis, and drop in a 315-horsepower version of AMC's 390-cubic-inch engine. To differentiate these cars from the pedestrian Ramblers that drove the nursing home set mad with automotive lust, Hurst gave the car one of the most outspoken paint schemes of the entire muscle car era. The red-and-white car, called the SC/Rambler/Hurst, featured a blue stripe across the roof and rear deck. The stripe began with an arrow on the hood pointing to the huge, blocky hood scoop, with the phrase "390 CU-IN" at the base of the arrow head.

The cheap ($3,000), light SC/Rambler was a rocket, easily capable of turning in quarter-mile times in the mid-14-second bracket. With a few Group 19 parts, it could break into the 12-second bracket. After the first batch of 500 sold out, Hurst built a second run of 500 cars, this time with toned-down paint. Some AMC dealers had been so offended by the outrageous paint of the original that they refused to put the cars on their lots. Realizing that such attitudes contributed heavily to AMC's financial woes, when the company ordered a third batch of SC/Ramblers it specified the original paint scheme.

In all, AMC sold 1,512 SC/Ramblers. It wasn't enough to save the Rambler nameplate, but at least it sent the old man off in style.

Yenko built just 99 Chevelles in 1969, making the Yenko Chevelle rarer than the Yenko Camaro, which had a production run of 201 cars that same year.

American Motors teamed up with George Hurst to produce the 1969 Hurst SC/Rambler, a Rambler with a 390-cubic-inch V-8 built by Hurst Performance.

TOO MUCH, TOO LATE

The 390 engine in the Hurst SC/Rambler generated a mere 315 horsepower, but a curb weight of just 3,000 pounds gave the cars a high power-to-weight ratio that put it among the quickest of all muscle cars available in 1969.

By 1970, everyone in the automotive industry knew the muscle car era was coming to an end. Smog, which was a slang term for "smoky fog," had become a major health concern in metropolitan areas. The federal government had taken action to curb the air pollution that was choking American cities, and this action had the support of the majority of the American people. President Richard Nixon created the Environmental Protection Agency (EPA), a federal department that sniffed out sources of smog and tried to eliminate them. As a major source of smog creating pollutants, passenger cars became a primary focus of the EPA's attention. The federal government began requiring increasingly stringent emissions control equipment on cars, equipment that robbed the engines of power. To maintain higher power levels, engines grew larger.

The Hurst SC/Rambler's loud red-white-and-blue color scheme frightened timid AMC dealers; some refused to put the cars on their lots.

In 1970, General Motors relented and let Chevrolet mount its largest big-block engine in the Chevelle. By this time the motor had grown to 454 cubic inches.

In 1970, Chevrolet raised the displacement of its biggest big-block to 454 cubic inches through an increased stroke. The bore on the original Mark II racing engine was about as big as the block could handle from the beginning of its development. Increasing the stroke was the only option for building a larger engine with any reliability. Rather than casting a taller block, as Chrysler had done with the 383 B block to create the 440 RB block, Chevrolet engineers installed a crankshaft with a longer throw. Motorcyclists had used this trick to increase the displacement of Harley-Davidson motorcycle engines for years. Other than an increased stroke, Chevy engineers didn't change much when converting the 427 engines to 454 cubic inches. Even the camshafts of the various engine packages remained virtually unchanged. The LS4, the basic package that went in passenger cars and trucks, was rated at 345 horsepower. The LS5 had a hotter camshaft and produced 360 horsepower. The hottest version, the one everyone wanted to have powering their Chevy muscle car, was the LS6 version, rated at 450 horsepower and a massive 500 ft-lb of torque. This engine featured different heads than the LS5, with square ports and mechanical lifters operating large valves, which fed 11.5:1 compression pistons through a high-rise aluminum intake manifold. Only 4,475 Chevelle buyers ordered LS6 engines in 1970.

Muscle car sales declined across the board in 1969. General Motors' offerings had suffered even greater sales drops than had the big-engined cars from rivals Chrysler and Ford. When faced with a choice between protecting customers from themselves and losing money or giving the market what it seemed to want, GM's management chose the bottom line over what it believed to be the greater good. For 1970, management allowed its divisions to mount their biggest engines in their intermediate-sized muscle cars.

The most potent version of the 454-cubic-inch V-8 was the LS-6, which generated 450 horsepower and 500 ft-lb of torque.

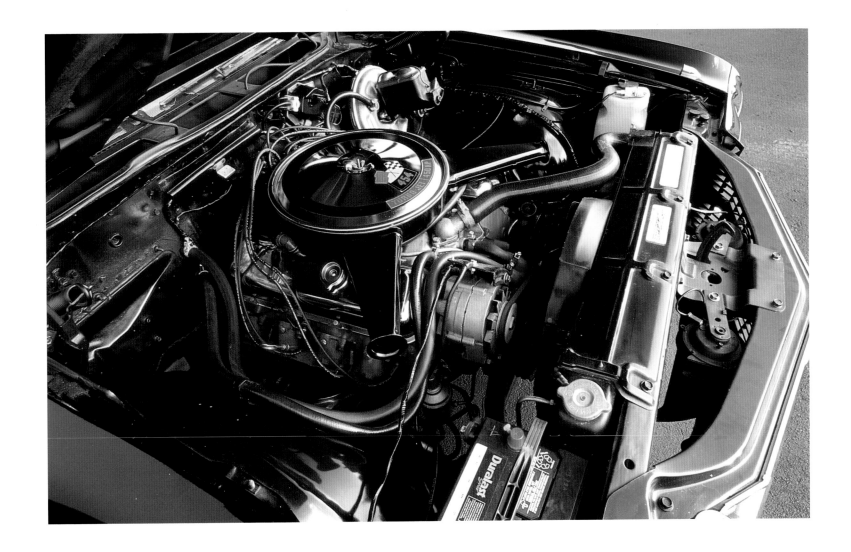

Chevelle buyers could equip any SS model with the LS-6 454 in 1970—even the convertible.

Chevrolet made the 454-cubic-inch V-8 available on the Chevelle-based El Camino SS pickup in 1970. With forward weight bias, the vehicles weren't the fastest at the drag strip, but they could certainly light up the rear tires.

Chevrolet responded to this newfound freedom by stuffing the new 454-cubic-inch engine under the Chevelle's hood. When composing the list of regular production options for the 1970 Chevelle, the division saw fit to include the 450-horsepower LS6 version of the big engine. If a Chevelle buyer could scrape up an additional $1,004.36 to add regular production option Z15 to his car's build sheet, he could drive off with one of the most iconic cars of the entire muscle car era.

The LS6-equipped 1970 Chevelle SS454 was also one of the fastest cars of the era and its engine the most powerful to propel any regular production Chevrolet. Even the most ham-fisted magazine tester could get the car into the 13-second bracket on stock tires, and with the right driver and the right tires, 12-second times were possible. This was a regular production Chevrolet that would run with the COPO cars and the dealer specials.

By the time this 1971 Monte Carlo SS hit the road, its 454 V-8 had been detuned thanks to lower compression ratios.

In addition to the Chevelle and El Camino, Chevrolet offered the 454 V-8 as an option for the more luxurious Monte Carlo.

When Oldsmobile began offering 455-cubic-inch V-8s as regular production options, it simply had to drill larger holes in the 401-cubic-inch engine, which was already just a sleeved down 455.

The LS6 was listed as an option in 1971, but none were produced. That year General Motors ordered its divisions to lower compression ratios across the board. The EPA had warned U.S. automakers that it was soon going to ban the use of tetraethyl lead as an additive in gasoline. Lead had been added to gasoline since before World War II to prevent engine detonation, allowing the use of higher compression ratios. Leaded fuel technology reached maturity during the war, allowing fighter and bomber aircraft engine makers to develop much more power, but lead was a nasty carcinogenic substance that caused birth defects, mental retardation, and all sorts of problems with the environment, though its role in these problems wasn't clearly understood at the time. What was known was that the EPA planned to institute emissions requirements beginning in 1975 that would require most automakers to install catalytic converters in their exhaust systems. These converters used platinum-coated beads to reduce the toxic emissions in automotive exhaust. Lead contaminated these beads and plugged up the converters. General Motors decision to reduce compression

levels was the first step in preparing its passenger cars for the upcoming catalytic converters and the lower-octane gasoline their use would mandate. In 1971, the LS6 engine, which was installed in just 188 Corvettes, only lost 25 horsepower. The big engine would lose far more power before General Motors started installing converters for the 1975 model year. The coming of the catalytic converter meant the classic muscle car era would soon be over.

In the meantime, Chevrolet was determined to produce the best muscle cars it had ever built. The same was true for other General Motors divisions. When word came down from on high proclaiming that GM's muscle cars would finally have engines equal to or better than those of their competitors, Oldsmobile had no problems mounting its 455-cubic-inch engine in the division's 4-4-2. Since 1968 the 4-4-2 had featured a 400-cubic-inch engine that was simply a 455 with reduced cylinder bores.

In 1969 Olds had introduced its W-30 option for the 4-4-2. In addition to improved suspension components, this package consisted of a plastic hood with functional air

Oldsmobile offered a W-30 package for its 4-4-2 muscle cars, consisting of improved suspension components, a plastic hood with functional air induction, a hotter camshaft, higher compression, and a larger carburetor.

INSET: Power ratings for the W-30 engine fell to 350 horsepower in 1971, thanks to a drop in compression ratio.

induction, a hotter camshaft, higher compression, and a larger carburetor. Olds rated the 400-cubic-inch W-30 at 360 horsepower. In 1970, Oldsmobile applied this same treatment to the 455-cubic-inch version of the W-30 package. The extra 55 cubic inches of displacement only brought a 10 horsepower increase in the power rating, but this was more a result of Oldsmobile's desire to fool insurance companies than any tendencies toward under-achievement of the W-30 engine. Artificially low horsepower ratings were becoming almost standard practice for muscle car manufacturers. Insurance companies were starting to exert a negative influence on muscle car sales. The equation of high-horsepower, low-weight cars plus young male drivers yielded the sum of exorbitantly high insurance premiums. While many baby boomers could afford the relatively low prices the manufacturers charged for muscle cars, they were starting to have problems affording the steep costs of insuring the beasts.

The 1970 4-4-2 with Oldsmobile's optional W-30 package generated 370 horsepower, a claim that was intentionally low to fool insurance companies.

Pontiac's Judge featured the division's 400-cubic-inch, 360-horsepower Ram Air III V-8 as standard equipment. An optional 370-horsepower Ram Air IV was available.

Realizing that sales of Plymouth's popular Road Runner were cutting into GTO sales, Pontiac responded with its own cartoonish muscle car in 1969: the Judge.

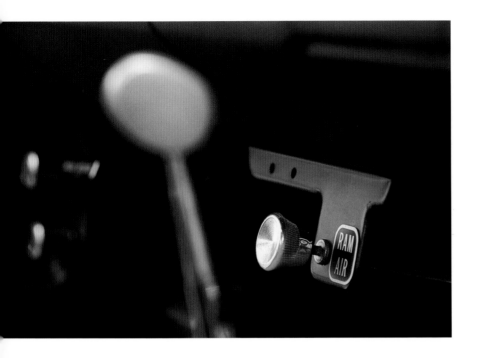

By 1969, GTO owners no longer had to install the Ram Air ducting system themselves, and remove it during wet weather; they simply had to push a button inside the cab to activate the fresh-air system.

Oldsmobile had built one of the finest interpretations of the muscle car concept with the 1970 4-4-2. It provided exceptional power, in spite of the low horsepower rating the manufacturer gave it, and it was one of the best handling of all the A-body cars from General Motors, but sales disappointed the division. Olds sold 33,607 4-4-2 models when the car was redesigned for 1968. When GM management finally allowed the division to bore the engine out to full strength in 1970, sales fell to just 19,330 units. The following year sales fell to just 7,589 units.

Part of the problem was that the A-body design that had seemed so fresh and contemporary in 1968 was starting to look dated, but a larger problem was that the classic muscle car era was coming to an end. Gas prices were rising, insurance was becoming prohibitively expensive, and the big-motored intermediates were turning into dinosaurs. Also, the market was changing. The Vietnam War raged throughout President Nixon's first term, and the young men who formed the bulk of muscle car buyers continued to be shipped to the other side of the planet by the hundreds of thousands. No industry can withstand a half-million potential customers from its prime demographic group being removed from the market at any given time without experiencing drastic changes.

Another factor in the impending demise of the classic muscle car era was the fact that baby boomers were aging. The bulge of customers that had been in their teens and early twenties when the muscle car market exploded were now in their late twenties and early thirties. More often than not, they had families of their own to support. The Mustang had been the perfect car for these people in the previous decade. Now they needed something a bit more practical for hauling the kids to football practice.

"HERE COMES DA JUDGE"

When Pontiac introduced the restyled GTO in 1968, it paid very little attention to its rivals at Chrysler's Plymouth division. In 1967 Plymouth offered just one entrant into the muscle car market: the GTX. The GTX was an extremely capable car, especially when equipped with the optional Hemi, but it wasn't a car that resonated with younger buyers. As Pontiac prepared the new GTO for its 1968 debut, it didn't consider Plymouth's 1968 offerings a major source of competition. After Plymouth sold nearly 50,000 of its Road Runner cartoon cars that year, Pontiac realized that it had underestimated the company.

Pontiac named the Judge after a skit on the popular television program *Laugh-In*.

The first GTO Judge models Pontiac produced were painted Carousel Red, which was the same color as Chevrolet's Hugger Orange. After February 1969, the Judge could be ordered in any GTO color, though Carousel Red was still the most popular.

Pontiac General Manager John DeLorean formed a committee to brainstorm ideas for the 1969 model year. DeLorean asked advertising executive Jim Wangers to sit on the committee. One of the challenges the committee faced was developing Pontiac's answer to the Road Runner, which had cut into GTO sales. Focusing on Plymouth's initial marketing of the Road Runner as a low-priced muscle car, the committee originally devised a car called the E/T, a budget-priced GTO with a hopped-up 350-cubic-inch engine. While this car could beat a 383-equipped Road Runner through the quarter-mile, DeLorean was less than happy with the committee's engine choice. In *Glory Days*, Wangers describes DeLorean's response when first seeing the car:

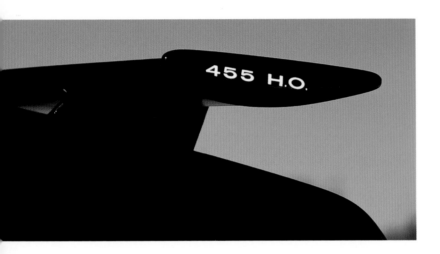

> During our one-hour delivery, he sat stone-faced, not saying a word and never changing expression. At the conclusion, he looked at us all and said, very coolly, "Over my dead body. Don't you guys know this is a 400 cubic inch world? As long as I have anything to say about it, there will never be a GTO with anything less than a 400 cubic inch engine. I recognize what you are trying to do, and I support the concept, but get that !@#!*% 350 out of that car!" He had our attention, to say the least. He concluded his statement: "Bring this car up to GTO standards and then we'll figure out how to cut the price."

When General Motors allowed Pontiac to use engines larger than 400 cubic inches in the GTO, the division retained the 400 Ram Air IV, rated at 370 horsepower, as the top performance engine. The 455 H.O. was rated at just 360 horsepower.

This forced the committee to entirely rethink its approach. DeLorean's edict made sense—initially the Road Runner had been marketed as a budget-priced car but most buyers had loaded it up with enough options to bring the price up to GTO levels. The committee began adding standard equipment to the new package, transforming it from the least expensive GTO into the most expensive GTO. They made the 366-horsepower Ram Air III engine standard equipment and the Ram Air IV engine, conservatively rated at 370 horsepower, was the only optional engine. The Ram Air IV option put the GTO on par with a 440-Six-Pack-equipped Road Runner when it came to quarter-mile times.

When the committee showed the revised car to DeLorean, he liked the upscale concept, still called the E/T. In *Glory Days*, Wangers describes DeLorean's reaction:

> Clearly, he was more pleased with this new GTO concept. "All right guys, I'll buy the car." His smile broadened (as did ours). "But, let's forget about that silly name." Oh no, I thought, another DeLorean bombshell!

"Every time I turn on the TV these days," DeLorean continued, "I hear this funny guy shouting, 'Here comes da Judge, Here comes da Judge!' So let's give them their damn Judge!" DeLorean, like many other people in late-1960s America, was a big fan of the popular NBC-TV show *Rowan and Martin's Laugh-In*. That "funny guy" shouting "Here comes da Judge!" was a young "Flip" Wilson.

From that moment on, our new car was "The Judge."

Buick restyled the Gran Sport for 1970. More importantly, the car received a potent 455-cubic-inch V-8. In GSX trim with a Stage I package, this engine generated a massive 510 ft-lb of torque.

Like all GM muscle cars, Buick lowered the compression ratio of the GSX in 1971.

In 1969 Chrysler attempted to pursue success in NASCAR stock car racing through aerodynamic improvements and introduced the Charger 500.

The Judge succeeded in its intended mission of raising the GTO's profile in an increasingly crowded muscle car market. Perhaps it succeeded too well. Pontiac had difficulty filling all the orders it received, which caused problems with the division's dealer network. At the end of 1969, Pontiac had sold 6,833 Judges, nearly 10 percent of the 72,287 GTOs it sold that year.

In 1968, when DeLorean had told the committee that it was a 400-cubic-inch world, he was guilty of understatement. In truth, the auto industry was well on its way to becoming a 440-plus-cubic-inch world. When GM management finally decided to enter the mega-cubic-inch engine frenzy in 1970, Pontiac found the transition a bit more difficult than Oldsmobile, which already had a sleeved-down 455-cubic-inch V-8 engine powering its A-body muscle cars. The largest engine Pontiac offered in any of its cars in 1969 displaced 428 cubic inches. There was no way the performance division was going to let rival Oldsmobile have a larger engine in its muscle car, so Pontiac's engineers increased both the bore and the stroke of the 428 to create a 455-cubic-inch monster motor.

The primary aerodynamic improvements to the Charger 500 consisted of flush-mounted glass and a flush-mounted grill. It wasn't enough—Ford's even more aerodynamic car, the Torino Talladega, won the Daytona 500 in 1969.

After getting beaten by Ford at the 1969 500-mile NASCAR race in Daytona, Chrysler went back to the wind tunnel, emerging with the single most outrageous muscle car of all time: the Charger Daytona.

The most distinctive feature of the Charger Daytona was its giant upright rear wing. The wing only needed to rise 12 inches above the rear deck to provide sufficient downforce, but designers mounted it 23 inches high to allow room for opening the trunk lid.

At least everyone expected Pontiac to produce a monster motor. Instead, the division left the 370-horsepower Ram Air IV engine as the top performance engine in the GTO, reasoning that with its shorter stroke the higher-revving 400-cubic-inch Ram Air IV would provide livelier performance. Pontiac rated the new 455 HO option at just 360 horsepower and marketed it on the strength of its 500 ft-lb of torque. After internalizing the "more-horsepower-is-better" mantra for a generation, the market did not buy Pontiac's logic, and GTO sales fell nearly 50 percent in 1970. For 1971 Pontiac relented and used the freer-flowing round-port heads from the Ram Air IV package in the 455 HO, but by this time it was too late. General Motors management had ordered its divisions to reduce compression ratios in all their engines to prepare for the coming of unleaded, lower-octane gasoline,

The 18-inch plastic snout on the Charger Daytona reduced frontal area and provided downforce at the speeds generated on NASCAR's superspeedways. The winged Chryslers were clocked on track at nearly 250 miles per hour.

and the 1971 455 HO put out just 335 horsepower. Pontiac had missed a very brief window in which the division had the opportunity to produce the killer GTO of all time.

General Motors' conservative Buick division had been a bit quicker to capitalize on this opportunity in 1970, producing one of the greatest muscle cars ever built. That year the Gran Sport received aesthetically pleasing bodywork, ditching the bizarre accent crease along its side that gave it the profile of a surly Norwegian bachelor farmer. More importantly, it received one of the great engines of the muscle car era.

A quick glance at the spec sheet didn't reveal the 455-cubic-inch engine's greatness. The engine's 350-horsepower rating fell below the ratings of its big-engined competitors, but given the artificially low ratings of the period, this number had little relationship to the engine's actual output. To get an idea of how underrated the engine was, consider that the same engine in the same state of tune was rated at 370 horsepower when mounted in the Buick Riviera, and even that rating was low. True horsepower output exceeded 400 ponies. But like the engines powering earlier versions of the GS, the 1970 GS455 engine wasn't about peak horsepower. The GS455 had one of the highest torque ratings of any engine ever to power a muscle car: 510 ft-lb of the twisting force. This is enough torque, according to the late astrophysicist and muscle car fanatic Carl Sagan, to measurably change the earth's rotation.

Starting in 1970, Buick offered a GSX package for the GS455 consisting of a 455-cubic-inch Stage I engine rated at 360 horsepower and some cosmetic upgrades. This car was Buick's answer to Pontiac's Judge. The car was quick as hell, capable of breaking into the 13-second quarter-mile bracket with the right tires, but unlike Pontiac, Buick put almost no effort into promoting the package. Buick built fewer than 1,000 GSX models, including a miniscule run produced at the beginning of the 1972 model year.

The interior was one place the street versions of the winged Chryslers differed from their racing brethren. The street versions were as luxurious as any Mopar muscle car.

MOPAR, THE NEXT GENERATION

In 1970 one didn't need to be a professional clairvoyant with the supernatural ability to scry into a crystal ball to see that the muscle car era was ending, but Chrysler was on a roll and continued to develop ultra-high-performance machines. Chrysler intended to build its powerful street fighters until the federal government pried the last Hemi from its corporate fingers.

Much of Chrysler's single-minded focus on performance came about as a result of the company's determination to regain the NASCAR Grand National championship from Ford. Like Ford, Chrysler had developed its racing Hemi about as far as possible, given the technological limitations of the day. And like Ford, any increase in performance would have to come through increases in aerodynamic efficiency. In 1968, Chrysler's designers took the aerodynamically awful Dodge Charger into the wind tunnel and began crafting a car as slippery as the Ford Torino and Mercury Cyclone twins. The most notable features of the car that resulted from this work, the Charger 500, were a flush-mounted front grille and a flush-mounted rear window in place of the tunnel-type rear window used on the regular production Charger. Though stylish, this tunnel contributed to terrible airflow over the car and held down top speeds on NASCAR track.

When Chrysler brought out a new 'Cuda in 1970, it used the cowl from the upcoming redesign of its B-body muscle cars, enabling the new pony car to use any engine in Chrysler's stable, including the mighty Hemi.

The new-for-1970 'Cuda was joined by an E-body pony car from Dodge: the Challenger. When equipped with a Hemi, the only thing preventing the powerful engine from twisting a convertible E-body frame into a trapezoid was the lack of traction provided by the skinny 70-series tires.

With the Charger 500, Chrysler took a much-improved aerodynamic package to Daytona for the running of the 1969 Daytona 500. Unfortunately for Chrysler, Ford presented an even more aerodynamic version of the Torino and Cyclone couplet, the Torino Talladega and the Cyclone Spoiler. The Ford cars used the same basic aerodynamic tricks as the Charger 500—flush grille, flush-mounted glass—to greater effect. A Ford Talladega won the 500 that year.

At this point Chrysler declared all-out war on Ford, as well as any other company impudent enough to challenge Mopar supremacy on NASCAR's superspeedways. Its designers went back to the wind tunnel and emerged with the single most insane automobile of the entire muscle car era: the Dodge Daytona. At its front, the new Daytona featured an 18-inch prosthetic nose, designed to reduce frontal area and provide downforce at speed. In back, to balance the downforce up front, the car featured a

huge wing placed on 23-inch-tall uprights. To provide downforce in racing, the wing only needed to be raised 12 inches from the rear deck, but Dodge designers placed it almost twice that high to allow the trunk lid to open on street-going versions of the car. This aerodynamic package made the racing version of the car good for top speeds of nearly 250 miles per hour.

Only nine buyers equipped convertible Challengers with Hemi engines in 1970, making this one of the rarest of all American-made automobiles.

Plymouth created its own version of the winged car, the Superbird, later in the year. The Plymouth used a similar wing and nose, but had to improvise a bit on the roof design. Though the stock Road Runner had a more aerodynamically efficient rear window area than the stock Charger, the Charger's tunnel design lent itself to creating a more efficient fastback by simply covering the tunnel with a window. The rear sail area of the Road Runner had to be extended to create as efficient a design. To cover up the cobbled-together bodywork around the rear window, all Superbirds featured vinyl roof covers.

Both cars were built offsite by a company called Creative Industries, which had to hustle to build enough street-legal cars by the January 1, 1970, deadline to homologate the car for NASCAR racing for that year, but the results were worth the effort. The Mopars humiliated Ford on NASCAR tracks, winning 38 of 48 Grand National races. They would have won more, had tire technology been up to the speeds produced by the amazing winged cars, but it wasn't. Tire failure led to some of the hairiest crashes in NASCAR history. The combined threat of deadly crashes and total Chrysler domination led NASCAR's sanctioning body to ban the winged cars following the 1970 season.

The Hurst pistol-grip four-speed shifter available in the E-body cars didn't function well for drag racing–style speed shifts, but it looked so cool no one really cared.

The Hemi 'Cudas attract the most attention, but the examples equipped with the optional 440-Six Pack were nearly as quick and make much better street cars.

When Chrysler redesigned the B-body lineup for 1971, the winged cars disappeared. Since they were ineligible for NASCAR racing, there was little point in spending the money to develop winged versions of the new cars.

Dodge had not been neglecting its customers who wanted to drag race in its attempt to beat Ford in NASCAR racing. In 1969, it had followed Oldsmobile's lead and had contracted George Hurst to build a super hot rod version of its compact car, the Dart. Hurst built a handful of Dodge Dart GTS models with four-barrel versions of the 440-cubic-inch RB engines.

Like the Hemi, the 440 Six Pack had enough torque to fold the convertible E-body chassis into a pretzel, and examples are almost as rare today as convertibles with Hemi engines.

By the time the E-body cars hit the market in 1970, big spoilers rising up off the trunk lid were must-have accessories for any muscle car.

Like General Motors, Chrysler detuned most of its big-block V-8s for 1971. The Hemi was a notable exception, returning intact for one final year.

These cars, along with a handful of Plymouth Barracudas that featured the same engine, were built largely for promotional reasons and were not regular production options. Chrysler was still not a player in the lucrative pony car market. But Chrysler had big plans for changing all that. The corporation finally had a bit of extra cash with which to develop cars for the youth market, thanks to the success of its B-body intermediates. Chrysler designers took the cowl under development for the next generation B-body cars along with a number of other B-body chassis components to keep development costs down and built a pony car around them. Internally coded the "E-body," the car featured classic pony-car proportions—long hood, short deck, small passenger compartment. With its beautifully sculpted lines and purposeful stance, the car turned out to be one of the classic designs in all of automotive history.

When equipped with the 426 Hemi, the Challenger was one of the most fearsome muscle cars ever to roam the earth.

This face was not something anyone wanted to see in the rear-view mirror in 1971.

Plymouth campaigned its new E-body in Trans-Am racing in 1970, and built around 1,500 AAR 'Cuda homologation specials for the street. AAR stands for All American Racers, Dan Gurney's racing organization, which campaigned the 'Cuda in 1970.

Dodge's entrant in the SCCA's Trans-Am series was the Challenger T/A.

The car was actually a pair of cars: the Dodge Challenger and Plymouth Barracuda, introduced for the 1970 model year. The Dodge Challenger rode on a wheelbase that was stretched 2 inches over its Plymouth counterpart—112 inches versus 110 inches—and overall, the Dodge pony car was 4.3 inches longer than the Plymouth. This gave the Challenger more traditional proportions than the Barracuda, but it gave the Barracuda a more muscular stance. Technically they broke little new ground, but they did blur the line between pony car and muscle car. Because they used the basic front cowl from the impending B-body redesign, the new E-bodies were larger than their pony-car competitors from Ford or General Motors, but they were smaller than Chrysler's B-body muscle cars. Using B-body components also allowed Chrysler's engineers to mount any engine in the company's stable in the engine bays. This included the Hemi, which, when mounted in the new E-body cars, created the most potent muscle car package in the Mopar lineup.

Although offered in basic models with slant-six or 318-cubic-inch V-8 engines, the performance models of the cars were the ones that attracted the interest of muscle car fans. The sporty version of the 1970 Challenger was the R/T. The R/T featured the 383-cubic-inch B-block engine with Magnum heads as its base engine, though a buyer could chose an optional 440-cubic-inch engine with either a single four-barrel or three two-barrel carburetors. If that buyer wanted to have the fastest car in town, he could order the optional 426 Hemi. The performance version of the Barracuda was simply called the 'Cuda, and had the same selection of engines, with the addition of a high-performance 340-cubic-inch four-barrel-equipped engine. The smaller engine could be ordered as a no-cost option.

The street version of the E-body Trans-Am racers used 340-cubic-inch small-blocks topped by a trio of Holley two-barrel carburetors.

Like their racing counterparts, the E-body homologation specials featured side-exiting exhaust pipes. Unlike the racers, the street cars had functioning mufflers.

Chrysler introduced redesigned B-body cars for the 1971 model year. By the time the cars hit the streets the only big-block that retained its full strength was the Hemi, powering this Super Bee.

The redesigned 1971 Charger was also available with the Hemi, at least for one year.

The one engine option unique to the E-bodies came as standard equipment on a pair of special cars built to homologate the chassis for the SCCA Trans-Am racing series, which was still extremely popular in 1970. The engine was a 340-cubic-inch unit topped by three Holley two-barrel carburetors, and the cars were the AAR 'Cuda and the Challenger T/A. The T/A in the Challenger special's name stood for Trans-Am, obviously, but the AAR name is a bit less obvious to those not steeped in American racing history. The letters stood for All American Racers, the name of racing legend Dan Gurney's company. Chrysler and Gurney formed a partnership in 1969, an arrangement that saw Gurney heading Plymouth's factory Trans-Am racing team.

Chrysler's Trans-Am racing efforts met with limited success, but the homologation cars were home runs. The cars equipped with the high-revving small-block 340 engines handled much better than their big-block counterparts, because there was significantly less weight over the front wheels. In AAR and T/A forms the E-body cars received upgraded suspensions that further improved their handling, making them the best handling muscle cars

The year 1971 marked the final appearance of the mighty 426 Hemi. The world was about to enter an era that was decidedly unfriendly toward high-performance cars.

Chrysler ever produced. Though not on par with the monstrous big-blocks in sheer power output, the six-barrel-equipped 340s, conservatively rated at 290 horsepower, were faster than many of the big-block cars produced by the competition. Their lightweight fiberglass hoods proved to be delicate and prone to cracking and their side-exiting exhaust pipes could deafen a person on a long ride, but these were still some of the most desirable cars of the classic muscle car era.

Chrysler's last big money shot in the muscle car wars was its redesigned 1971 B-body platform. The new B-body models retained the Coke-bottle styling of the previous generation of cars, but adopted long-hood-short-deck pony-car proportions. Chrysler maintained the Charger, Super Bee, Road Runner, and GTX versions of the B-body chassis, but the Coronet

With the exit of the Hemi Road Runner after the 1971 model year, the traditional muscle car was nearly extinct.

R/T didn't make the cut. The killer big-block engines that had earned Mopar its legendary performance reputation all made the cut for 1971, including the Six-Pack versions of the 440 and the omnipotent 426 Hemi. Chrysler followed the lead of General Motors and reduced the compression ratio of the RB block engines for 1971 but held the line with the Hemi. That engine returned unchanged in 1971, making it the last original combatant standing in the muscle car battlefield.

In 1972, Chrysler further detuned its engines and the mighty 426 Hemi disappeared from the lineup. The B-body cars could still be ordered with big-block engines, but these engines struggled to put out as much power as the small-block engines of a few years earlier. The 340-cubic-inch engine was the top offering in the E-body cars for 1972; the big-block engine had disappeared from their option lists. Almost before anyone realized what was happening, one of the most exciting periods in automotive history had all but come to an end. ▥

Buyers of Mopar muscle cars could still get big-block engines in 1971, but they were less powerful than they had been the previous year, thanks to a drop in compression ratio.

CHAPTER 7
THE DEATH OF FUN AND THE RESURRECTED MUSCLE CAR

When Ford introduced the redesigned Mustang GT for the 2005 model year, it produced one of the highest-performing cars ever to wear the fabled name of the original pony car.

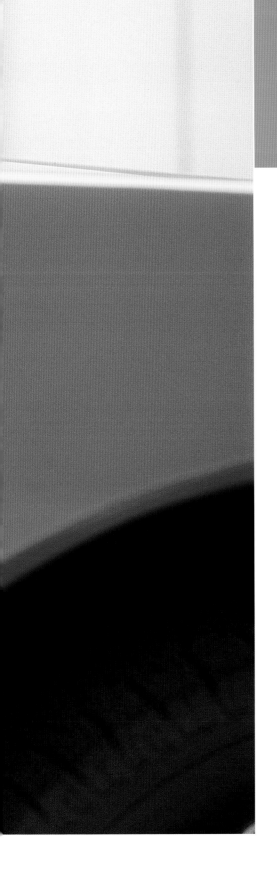

Pontiac unleashed the Super Duty 455 Trans Am and Formula on America in 1973, as a final act of defiance signaling the end of the classic muscle-car era.

T he year 1970 went down as the peak year for muscle car performance. Beginning in 1971, U.S. automakers began to detune their engines with lower compression, retarded ignition, milder camshafts, and increasingly restrictive intake and exhaust systems in an attempt to meet toughening pollution-control standards. Horsepower ratings began to drop, and would continue to

decrease for a generation. Chevrolet lowered the compression ratio of its engines in 1971 to cope with the removal of lead additives from gasoline. Horsepower of its LS6 454 fell from 450 to 425 that year, and would fall much more in coming years.

Part of the decrease in the horsepower ratings manufacturers applied to their engines involved the way in which they measured horsepower output. Prior to 1972, most American automakers rated their engines in terms of SAE (Society of Automotive Engineers) gross horsepower, which was measured using a blueprinted test engine running on a stand without accessories, mufflers, or emissions control devices. This did not provide an accurate

Chrysler's 340-cubic-inch small-block V-8 retained most of its performance in 1972. Its power drop was more a function of the switch from SAE Gross to SAE Net horsepower measurement methods. It still had enough power to make the lightweight A-body Duster a quick street machine.

measurement of the power output of an installed engine in a street car. Gross horsepower figures were also easily manipulated by carmakers. They could be inflated to make a car appear more muscular or deflated to appease corporate and insurance safety-crats or to qualify a car for a certain class of racing.

By 1972 U.S. carmakers quoted power exclusively in SAE net horsepower, which rated the power of the engine with all accessories and standard intake and exhaust systems installed. This provided a more accurate measurement of a given car's potential, but the overall numbers were lower. Even engines that had received no mechanical changes or additional emissions-control equipment suddenly had lower horsepower ratings in 1972. For example, a 1971 Plymouth 'Cuda equipped with a 340-cubic-inch four-barrel was rated at 275 SAE gross horsepower. The same car with no significant mechanical changes was rated at 240 SAE net horsepower in 1972. The 35-horsepower drop was almost entirely due to the different measurement method. To this day, the 1972–1973 versions of the 340-four-barrel engines have reputations as "smog motors," even though they are virtually identical to the 1970–1971 engines.

The psychological effect this had on what was left of the muscle car buying public was a final nail in the coffins of these cars. This was a time before online communities argued ad nauseum about the merits of different brands of valve springs. It was before the Internet, before cable television even, and geniune information was hard to come by. Most hot rodders operated in a fog of misinformation and old wives' tales. People believed the power ratings printed in advertising brochures because often this was the only information available regarding power output. The average buyer didn't know SAE gross from SAE net; he only knew that the horsepower number had suddenly become smaller, and bigger was better than smaller. As a result, some very quick cars built between 1972 and 1974 earned undeserved reputations as underpowered.

As bad as this was, it wasn't the worst thing to happen to the market for high-performance cars. If an aging demographic, Draconian insurance premiums, and increasing encroachment by the federal government weren't enough to kill off muscle cars, the 1973 oil crisis was. This began on October 17, 1973, when Arab members of the Organization of Petroleum Exporting Countries (OPEC) announced that they would no longer ship petroleum to nations that had supported Israel in its conflict with Egypt, which meant the United States and its allies in Western Europe. The effects of the embargo were immediate, and the price of oil quadrupled by 1974. The embargo ended on March 17, 1974, but the aftermath would have a chilling effect on the performance-car market well into the next decade.

PONTIAC'S FINAL EXPLETIVE

By 1973 it seemed to everyone that the muscle car era was dead and gone. Chrysler's Hemi had disappeared, and Chevrolet's 454 was a faint shadow of its former self. When GM management ordered its divisions to drop compression ratios on all their engines, muscle car sales plummeted. GTO sales fell from 40,149 in 1970 to 10,532 in 1971. The year 1972 saw an even more drastic decrease in power output from the big engines along with a corresponding decrease in sales. Discounting the measurement differences created by the change from SAE gross to SAE net, Oldsmobile's 455-cubic-inch engine lost 50 horsepower in 1972. The classic muscle car era appeared to be over. But Pontiac, the brand that had kicked off the muscle car movement in the first place, wasn't about to roll over in submission and urinate on its soft corporate underbelly just yet. In a final act of defiance, the division thrust one last mighty middle finger in the face of the automotive

After 1969 the convertible Trans Am disappeared. Convertible tops upset the delicate sensibilities of the safetycrats as much as high-performance engines did.

The 1970 Trans Am equipped with a 345-horsepower Ram Air IV 400 was still a fierce muscle car.

By 1973 most pundits had declared the muscle car era over. Imagine their surprise when Pontiac unleashed the new Super Duty Firebird.

establishment. In 1973, when every other manufacturer had jumped the sinking high-performance ship, Pontiac built something that everyone else thought impossible: a true muscle car.

By this time the last performance car in Pontiac's lineup was the Firebird. The GTO was just a sad option on the restyled LeMans model. The following year it would migrate to the Ventura, Pontiac's version of the lowly Nova, and after that disappear for the next two decades. The sportiest Pontiacs were the Formula and Trans Am Firebirds. The Trans Am package had debuted midway through the 1969 model year, the last year

In case you haven't noticed, Pontiac's '73 Firebirds are here.

We build four different kinds. For people who take driving excitement seriously. The question is…how serious do you want to get?

Trans Am: As serious as they come.
It's the red one above. See how serious it is? Everything functional. The spoilers spoil. The air dams dam. That's why a lot of folks rank it as the best performing Yank on the road.
A 455-cubic-inch, 4-bbl. V-8 with a 4-speed manual transmission is standard. And there's a new Super

Duty 455-cubic-inch V-8 available.
No, the giant bird on the hood isn't functional. It's not standard, either. You have to order it. But…!

Formula: Two scoops, three flavors.
The two scoops you can see on the hood above. The flavors are a 350 V-8, a 400 V-8, a 455 V-8. Order the Formula 'Bird as you see fit.
The new interior is all business.
So are the standard front disc brakes and the handling package you can order.

While the scoops look tough, the toughest part of any Firebird is the front bumper. It's made of Endura to help fight dents and dings. And it's been reinforced this year to make it stronger.

Esprit: Can a sports car be luxurious?
Esprit wipes out all doubt. The new bucket seats, the new cloth or all-vinyl upholstery, the new instrument panel and door trim are as plush as you'll find in many a luxury car.
The ride's almost that plush, too.

Basic Firebird: What we didn't sacrifice for price.
This is our easiest to own Firebird.
You still get molded foam bucket seats; loop-pile carpeting; High-Low ventilation; the Endura bumper; a strong, double-shell roof that absorbs sound; Firebird's futuristic styling and outstanding handling.
That's our way with sports cars. Are you ready to get serious?

Buckle up for safety.

The Wide-Track people have a way with cars.

Though rated at only 290 horsepower, the Super Duty Pontiacs of 1973 and 1974 were measured using the new SAE net measurement methods. To get a better idea of just how strong the engines were, the Super Duties put out the same SAE net torque measurements—390 ft-lb—as the mighty 426 Hemi. These were true muscle cars.

of Pontiac's original Camaro-derived F-car. Even though the name "Trans Am" implies that the car was designed for the SCCA's Trans-American Sedan Racing series, the car was built for the street and never homologated for racing. The name just sounded cool.

In 1970 Pontiac introduced a redesigned Firebird. This redesign allowed Pontiac to build the F-car it had always wanted to build, and the new Firebird quickly earned a reputation for killer handling, especially in Trans Am trim. In addition to sporty body-work and stripes, the Trans Am package included a number of suspension improvements. The top engine in the 1970 car was a 345-horsepower, 400-cubic-inch Ram Air IV, similar to the top engine offered in that year's GTO.

As with the GTO, Firebird power levels started to drop in 1971. That year Pontiac offered a low-compression version of the 455 HO with an SAE gross horsepower rating of 335 as an optional engine in the Trans Am. Horsepower ratings fell again in 1972, though Pontiac used the better-breathing round-port heads to help compensate for the power drained off by new emissions control equipment. Power appeared to fall yet again in 1973, but that was the case only for those living in the rarified world of numbers on paper. In the real world, 1973 marked a resurgence of Pontiac performance, in the form of the Super Duty 455 option available on the Formula and Trans Am versions of the Firebird.

Pontiacs had always featured opulent interiors and the Super Duty Firebird interior was no exception.

The SD455 engine combined every high-performance piece remaining in Pontiac parts catalog—radical camshaft, big carburetor, four-bolt main-bearing caps, forged connecting rods, aluminum flat-top pistons—in a last-ditch effort not to let the encroaching nanny state strangle the fun out of performance cars. With a low 8.4:1 compression ratio, the engine was only rated at 290 horsepower, not, seemingly, the stuff of which muscle car legends are made. But that horsepower rating told only part of the Super Duty story.

Consider this: While the SD455 was rated at only 290 horsepower, it was rated at 390 ft-lb of torque, and that was using the SAE net measurement. To put that figure in perspective, while a 426 Hemi had a SAE gross torque rating of 490 ft-lb, when measured using the SAE net method, that same engine generated 390 ft-lb of torque, as did the SD455. Any engine that generates as much torque as a 426 Hemi deserves a place in the pantheon of great motors. Without question the SD455 Firebirds were true muscle cars, as their 13-second quarter-mile times bear out.

Pontiac offered the Super Duty engine in both the Trans Am and the Formula Firebirds.

They were the last of the true muscle cars, as it turned out. Pontiac got a late start building SD455 Firebirds and only produced 396 examples in 1973. In 1974 Pontiac built 943 SD455 Formulas and Trans Ams before the engine fell victim to the OPEC-induced oil shock. After that, the Super Duty engine disappeared from Pontiac's option list and with it the last of the true big-engine muscle cars. Pontiac would continue trying to maintain its reputation as GM's performance division, producing some admirable cars along the way. Pontiac engineers managed to massage 220 horsepower from the 400-cubic-inch engine used in the 1978 Trans Am, and even resorted to turbo charging when it was forced to scale back to a small 301-cubic-inch engine for the 1980 Trans Am. But they were fighting a losing battle. It would be nearly two decades before performance once again rose to SD455 levels.

With an engine that cranks out as much torque as a 426 Hemi, laying long, dark strips of rubber is child's play.

Buick offered a Gran Sport with a Stage 1 engine, but that engine managed to generate just 270 horsepower from 455 cubic inches.

FAUX MUSCLE

Following the demise of the SD455, the performance car market in the United States entered its Dark Ages. After offering a series of huge-displacement engines that generated embarrassingly small amounts of horsepower—imagine a 455-cubic-inch engine that produced just 160 ponies—the big motors disappeared. Various manufacturers attempted to stir interest in the youth market by putting legendary nameplates like "Road Runner," "4-4-2," and "Cobra" on lowly econocars and pimped-out personal luxury cars, but no one cared anymore.

Oldsmobile had a few good years in the late 1970s. With their crushed-velour interiors and vinyl landau tops, Oldsmobile built the right car for the times. The late 1960s had been defined by excessive automobile abuse; the late 1970s were defined by excessive self-abuse. Oldsmobile's Cutlass, the best-selling intermediate-sized car of the era, with its brothel-on-wheels persona, provided an ideal atmosphere in which to snort cocaine, the drug of choice at the time.

Pontiac generated some excitement with its 400-cubic-inch Trans Am in 1978, but the 220-horsepower car was just a faint echo of the SD455 version offered a few years earlier. Still, it was a damned sight better than the dreadful cars offered by Pontiac's competitors.

With a standard 455-cubic-inch engine generating just 275 horsepower, the 1973 Hurst/Olds was about appearance, not performance.

The Fury-based Road Runner sold poorly and few examples exist today. In this case rarity does not lead to value, and these cars do not command high prices among collectors.

INSET: In 1975 Plymouth produced a Road Runner based on its Fury luxury-coupe platform.

In a damning indictment of the state of the American auto industry in 1979, the most powerful muscle car produced that year was a pickup: Dodge's Li'l Red Express truck, to be precise.

In what was perhaps the most damning indictment of the U.S. auto industry at the time, the most muscular car of 1979–1980 wasn't even a car, it was a pickup truck. It was Dodge's Li'l Red Express truck, to be precise. With its gaudy red-and-gold paint and outrageous Peterbilt smokestack exhaust, the Li'l Red Express continued Chrysler's long-standing tradition of building cartoonish cars. But unlike other so-called performance cars of that time, which were mere caricatures of the muscle cars of old, the Li'l Red Express had a pair. A huge Carter Thermoquad four-barrel carburetor fed the 360-cubic-inch engine through a high-rise intake manifold. With an 8.2:1 compression ratio, the engine produced 225 horsepower and 295 ft-lb of torque, enough to send the outrageous little pickup

Because the Li'l Red Express was a light truck, not a passenger car, Dodge didn't have to meet the strict emissions requirements it met with its car engines. As a result, the 360 Express in the Li'l Red Express was a genuine tire shredder, with 225 horsepower and 295 ft-lb of torque.

through the quarter-mile in 15 seconds. While it might not seem like much today, compare the Li'l Red Express' power output to that of the 1979 Trans Am. With the exception of a small run of cars using 220-horsepower 400-cubic-inch Pontiac engines leftover from 1978, the Trans Am's top engine offering for 1979 was a 403-cubic-inch Oldsmobile engine that pumped out a pathetic 185 horsepower.

The Li'l Red Express was an entertaining hot rod. With all the weight over the front wheels, handling was abysmal, but the frontal weight bias meant that a seriously anti-social owner could put all the torque to good use. To this day, no one has ever built a vehicle that can burn through a pair of rear tires as quickly as the Li'l Red Express. Entertaining or not, the fact that a truck was the top-performing vehicle on the market in 1979 illustrates the incredible malaise the U.S. auto industry was in at the end of the 1970s.

With Kenworth-style smokestacks, one thing the Li'l Red Express most certainly was *not* was subtle.

BOOSTED BUICKS

Things began to look up for fans of high-performance automobiles in the 1980s. After years of limping along, the economy finally began to pick up and the price of gas began to fall. Automakers started to figure out how to meet emissions standards without sacrificing performance, and horsepower ratings began to rise. New technological developments like computerized ignition and fuel injection systems began to improve both performance and fuel economy. Forced induction systems, such as turbocharging and supercharging, led to significant increases in horsepower.

With the help of advanced technology, Buick made one last blip on the radar of muscle car fans in the 1980s. General Motors divisions had experimented with turbocharged engines since the dawn of the muscle car era. In 1962 Oldsmobile engineers had turbocharged a version of Buick's all-aluminum V-8 and installed it in Oldsmobile's F-85. Buick engineers continued to experiment with turbocharging, but such technology wouldn't appear on a production Buick until the 1978 model year.

The engine Buick boosted for its 1978 Regal was its venerable 231-cubic-inch V-6, a design it had developed in the 1960s, then sold to Jeep during the heyday of the muscle car era because there was little market for economical V-6 engines. In 1974, during the

In the mid-1980s Chrysler marketed a front-wheel-drive sporty car based on its K-car platform. The most sporting version of this new model was the Dodge Daytona Turbo Z.

The performance of the Turbo Z came from a turbo-charged 2.2-liter four-cylinder engine.

ASC/McLaren Specialty Products built the GNX for Buick.

INSET: Buick got back in the muscle car business in the 1980s with the turbo-charged Grand National GNX.

A Garret turbocharger pumped 15 pounds of boost into the GNX's 3.8-liter V-6 engine, resulting in 275 horsepower.

height of the gas crisis caused by the OPEC oil embargo, Buick bought the design back from Jeep and began updating it. The turbocharging system introduced for the 1978 model year was primitive, with an exhaust-driven air compressor drawing air through a carburetor, but when that carburetor was a four-barrel, the little engine produced 165 horsepower, as much as some of the huge-displacement V-8s of the day.

In 1982 Buick first called its Regal the Grand National, a nod to NASCAR's top stock car racing series. Originally the Grand National was just a cosmetic package for the Regal and didn't even use the turbocharged engine from the Regal T-type. Instead, it used a 125-horsepower, 4.1-liter version of the normally aspirated V-6. When the Grand National name returned for 1984, the car had something more to offer than just exciting trim. Not only did the 1984 Grand National use a turbocharged engine, it featured sequential fuel injection instead of carburetors. The addition of a modern fuel injection system made the turbocharged Buick engines much more tractable in daily driving and

In 1988, a Ford Mustang equipped with a 5.0-liter engine provided potent performance, but it was still saddled with an 85-mile-per-hour speedometer, a relic from the fuel crisis of the 1970s.

also much more powerful. A stock 1984 Grand National produced 200 horsepower, putting it on par with the small-block V-8s found in Camaros and Mustangs of the era.

In 1987 the division introduced the ultimate version of the Grand National, the one-year-only GNX. The GNX followed in the tradition of specialty cars built by outside firms, like the Shelby Mustangs and Hurst/Olds cars of the 1960s. Buick sent fully optioned Grand Nationals to ASC/McLaren Specialty Products, where they received more-efficient Garrett air-to-air intercoolers, front fender vents to pull away engine heat, and a special Garrett turbocharger that used a lightweight ceramic impeller. ASC/McLaren set maximum boost at 15 psi, bumping the horsepower output to 275. The company also beefed up the suspension and body structure, but the handling still wasn't on par with other performance cars of the day. One magazine wag writing for *Car and Driver* described the GNX as a great engine looking for a decent car. That great engine didn't come cheap, either. The GNX package added $11,000 to the base price, bringing the total cost of purchasing the car to $29,900.

The Buick turbos grew into true muscle cars by the time they disappeared, along with all the GM rear-wheel-drive intermediates following the 1987 model year. A stock GNX could turn in 13-second quarter-mile times. Today the cars have developed a cult status, in part because of what they were capable of when new, but mostly because of their potential. A stock GNX might have developed 275 horsepower, but with the addition of a few electronic components and a bit of fuel injection tweaking, the engines were capable of producing more than twice that much horsepower.

The LX version of the 1988 Mustang equipped with a High Output 5.0-liter engine made an excellent performance car for drivers wanting to keep a low profile.

THE REBIRTH OF MUSCLE

Ford's Mustang and Chevrolet's Camaro share responsibility for restarting the performance wars in Detroit. Beginning in the mid-1980s, competition between the two traditional pony cars caused horsepower ratings to begin climbing back up to acceptable levels.

General Motors redesigned its F-cars for 1982. Chevrolet's suspension engineers did such a good job with the Z/28 that it earned a reputation as the best-handling car built in America (at least until a redesigned Corvette appeared for the 1984 model year). It stole this title from rival Pontiac's Trans Am. At that time the Mustang couldn't compete with the Camaro when it came to handling. The Mustang had been redesigned in 1979, but the resulting car was based on what Ford called its Fox platform, the basic underpinning of such universally reviled cars as the Ford Fairmont Futura. When any amount of power was applied to this chassis, the rear end would hop like a 1962 Chevy II on methamphetamine.

Ford's engineers worked to solve the car's handling issues throughout the 25 years the Fox-based Mustang was in production. In 1984, Ford's Special Vehicle Operations (SVO) team made great strides toward taming rear-wheel hop when it introduced a revised rear suspension for the Mustang. Originally mounted on a special turbocharged Mustang called the SVO, this system used four shocks instead of two to control axle hop. When applied to the standard, Mustang it allowed the use of increasingly powerful V-8 engines.

Increasingly powerful V-8 engines were exactly what people wanted. The SVO was one of the sportiest American cars produced in the mid 1980s, but it was powered by a four-cylinder engine. Sure, the engine was turbocharged to produce 175 horsepower, but it was still a four-cylinder engine. Everyone knew that a proper muscle car needed a proper V-8 engine.

The High Output version of the Mustang's 5.0-liter engine produced 225 horsepower and 300 ft-lb of torque.

For 1993, GM restyled its F-cars once again. The Camaro adopted distinctively Japanese-looking lines, while the Firebird adopted a wild array of exaggerated curves and angles that all seemed to compete with one another for attention. When Ford redesigned its Mustang the following year, its designers did not follow GM's lead and adopt postmodern styling. Rather than looking to Japan for inspiration, as Chevrolet had done, or designing a vehicle that looked like a child's toy, as Pontiac had done, Ford mined its own rich heritage. The new Mustang combined a modern look with inspired elements from the car's past.

Performance-wise, the car was far from the equal of the new F-cars from General Motors. The new Mustang was just a reskinning of the old car, wart-like Fox chassis and

all. The 302-cubic-inch engine was tuned to produce 215 horsepower, roughly equal to the Camaro's high-output 305, but by that time General Motors was offering the new 350-cubic-inch LT-1 small-block V-8 engine developed for the Corvette in the F-body cars. This engine developed 275 horsepower in the Z/28, and some versions developed much more than that. The 1992 Firehawk SLP version of the Trans Am produced 350 horsepower and 390 ft-lb of torque. This 13-second quarter-mile terror was a true muscle car, though a very expensive one at $40,000.

Meanwhile the Mustang traded on its 215 horsepower and good looks. Magazine writers weren't especially kind to the new Mustang, preferring the more-powerful and better-handling pony cars from General Motors. Unfortunately for GM, magazine writers seldom buy cars of their own. They analyze cars with their heads. The buying public analyzes cars with their hearts. The new F-cars were superior to the Mustang by any empirical measurement—speed, handling, comfort—but the Mustang outsold the Camaro two-to-one and the Firebird three-to-one. Chevrolet, in part, suffered from the loss of its long-time

Ford redesigned the Mustang GT for 1987.

marketing manager, hot rodder Jim Perkins, who left Chevrolet to work for Hendrick Motorsports. Perkins would have approached the task of selling F-body cars the old-fashioned way: win on Sunday, sell on Monday.

For 1996, Ford introduced a new engine for the Mustang, a 281-cubic-inch V-8 that abandoned traditional pushrods for overhead cams. Initially the engine produced the same horsepower and torque as the aging 302 it replaced. By the decade's end it had been tuned to produce 260 horsepower. It was still no match for the top LS-1 engine, the all-aluminum 5.7 liter V-8 designed for the C5 Corvette, which made its way into the F-car engine bay for the 1998 model year. This high-tech pushrod V-8, the first all-aluminum engine in a Camaro since the 1969 ZL1, produced 305 horsepower in the Z28, and 320 horsepower in the SS model, which featured a functioning ram-air system. This same engine in the Trans Am produced 325 horsepower when equipped with Pontiac's Ram

Air package, but it no longer mattered. Sales of GM's pony cars had fallen to such dismal levels that the only things keeping them in the lineup were tradition and entropy. The year 2002 saw the death of both the Firebird and Camaro nameplates. Interest in the cars had fallen to such a low point that, like the Rambler before it, few people noticed when the cars finally shuffled off this mortal coil.

Unlike GM's F-cars, the Mustang continues to thrive. For 2005, Ford introduced an all-new Mustang with its first new chassis since Jimmy Carter was president. Based on the Lincoln LS platform, the most sophisticated rear-wheel-drive chassis in Ford's lineup, the new Mustang is, like the best pony cars of the past, a true muscle car. The current version of the OHC 281-cubic-inch power plant produces 300 horsepower and 320 ft-lb of torque, enough to propel the 3,600-pound Mustang through the quarter-mile in the high 13-second range. This makes the Mustang GT one of the fastest cars ever to carry that nameplate.

But Ford has even bigger plans for the Mustang. For 2007 it will resurrect the Shelby name and release the Shelby Cobra GT500. This car will be everything a Shelby has always been—handsome, brutally fast, exclusive—but it will also be the most civilized car ever to carry the Shelby name.

And it will be the fastest Mustang Ford has ever built. Power will come from a super-charged, 330-cubic-inch version of the Mustang's 281-cubic-inch unit, with some tweaks. The aluminum heads will carry a pair of camshafts above them rather than the single cam mounted atop the cast-iron heads on the standard Mustang GT. The Shelby cams will operate

Chevrolet reintroduced the Impala SS in 1994. This car featured a 260-horsepower 5.7-liter V-8 derived from the Corvette's LT-1.

In 2005, Ford introduced the first completely new Mustang since 1979.

32 valves, as opposed to the 24 found in the GT's three-valve cylinder heads. Most importantly, an Eaton Rootes–type supercharger will force-feed air into those cylinder heads, bringing total power up to an estimated 475 horses and 475 ft-lb of torque. Preproduction prototypes are regularly turning in 12-second quarter-mile times. And Ford hasn't neglected handling—like every car to carry the Shelby name, the new Cobra GT500 will have a suspension derived from racetrack experience.

Ford's Mustang isn't the only legendary muscle car nameplate left on the market. Pontiac revived the GTO for the 2004 model year. When Pontiac decided to revive its original muscle car concept, it had no rear-drive platform to which it could turn. While there are some great front-wheel-drive performance cars on the market, such cars are sport-compacts and not muscle cars. Even when you stuff a V-8 engine in them, as Pontiac has done with its current front-wheel-drive Grand Prix, they are not muscle cars. A muscle car needs to be able to create billowing plumes of smoke from the back tires; when those plumes come from the front of the car, it just looks like something has broken inside the engine. While Pontiac lacked a proper muscle car platform, Holden, General Motors' Australian division, had the Monaro, a great potential muscle car. In addition to delivering power

The 4.6-liter overhead cam engine powering the 2005 Mustang GT produced 300 horsepower and 320 ft-lb of torque.

The convertible Mustang disappeared during the 1970s, but reappeared in the 1980s and today is more popular than ever.

The new Mustang GT can blast through the quarter mile in the 13-second range, making it one of the fastest Mustangs ever.

to the correct pair of tires, the Monaro already had a true muscle car engine: the Corvette's LS-1. In Monaro trim the 350-cubic-inch engine produced 350 horsepower.

Pontiac added some GTO badges and a Pontiac-style front-end treatment, moved the steering wheel to the left, and brought the Monaro to the U.S. market as the Pontiac GTO. The 2004 GTO was a solid performer, but the car's appearance was nondescript at best. Pontiac's front-drive Grand Prix, by no means a stylish car, turned more heads than the plain-looking GTO. Even though the car was quick and handled better than any previous GTO, no one but Pontiac's advertising people called the new GTO "the Great One." Instead, they referred to it by the original GTO's other nickname: "the Goat." The cars sold as slowly as the last generation of Firebirds, and by the middle of the 2004 model year, dealers were discounting the car by 30 percent of their original retail price or more.

Ford introduced a new Shelby version of the Mustang for 2007: the Cobra GT500.

A supercharged, 5.4-liter version of Ford's overhead-cam V-8 powers the new Shelby.

For 2005, Pontiac designers made a few token efforts at giving the GTO more presence, like punching a couple of Ram Air–style holes in the hood and bolting a Judge-like wing to the rear deck, but there was only so much they could do with a car that looked like a coupe-version of the 1986 Ford Taurus.

The designers might have been hamstrung by the car's basic shape, but Pontiac's engineers had a terrific car to develop. The GTO already had a great suspension and a very good Corvette-derived engine. For 2005, Pontiac borrowed the new LS2 engine from the just-released C6 version of the Corvette and stuck it in the GTO. With this 364-cubic-inch, pushrod, two-valve-per-cylinder small-block V-8 that produced 400 horsepower and 400 ft-lb of torque, the GTO now had a great engine to match its chassis. The 3,800-pound car became a genuine 13-second-quarter-mile muscle car. The remarkable new LS2 engine proves that there is still life in the pushrod V-8 design. The new GTO may not have the visual flash of its illustrious GTO predecessors, but it's got enough muscle to spank each and every one of them in a stoplight drag race. Besides, as many people are finding out, nondescript looks aren't necessarily a bad thing for a car capable of going 160 miles per hour. Sometimes it's better not to draw too much attention to yourself, notwithstanding what product planners and many customers thought during the 1960s.

Pontiac isn't the only U.S. automaker getting back in the muscle car game. Dodge revived the Charger name for the 2006 model year, and the Chrysler division gave the car some serious muscle. In R/T form, the car is powered by a 350-horsepower Hemi. Once again the Hemi has been brought back from the dead. This 345-cubic-inch pushrod V-8 tops its fabled predecessor's SAE net horsepower rating and equals the 390 ft-lb of torque (SAE net) that the older 426 cubic-inch version produced.

But the new car has an even hotter version: The Charger SRT8 features a 370-cubic-inch Hemi that produces 425 horsepower and 420 ft-lb of torque. This modern Hemi produces net ratings that equal the old engine's gross ratings. The new Charger tears through the quarter-mile in the 13-second bracket, despite weighing a hefty 4,200 pounds.

Everyone expected Dodge to bring back the Charger. What no one expected was that the new car would have four doors. In the past, all muscle cars have had two doors, or possibly three if the car was a hatchback. Many people wonder if a four-door sedan can be a true muscle car. Apparently if it has a 425-horsepower Hemi and turns in 13-second quarter-miles, it can.

For those who refuse to accept a four-door muscle car, DaimlerChrysler has developed a modern rendition of Dodge's original pony car, the Challenger. (There will be no new 'Cuda, since DaimlerChrysler pulled the plug on the Plymouth brand after the 2001 model year.) The new Challenger is larger than its illustrious ancestor. Its 116-inch wheelbase is 6 inches longer than that of the original 1970 E-body challenger (8 inches longer than Plymouth's Barracuda) and it's overall length of 197.8 inches is almost 9 inches longer than the original car. (The new Challenger is over 11 inches longer than the original 'Cuda.) Even with larger proportions, Dodge designers have done a commendable job recreating the classic E-body look in a car with modern aerodynamic efficiency. Perhaps the most visible differences are the shorter front and rear overhangs on the new car and the modern low-profile rubber rolling on massive rims: 20-inches-by-9-inches up front and 21-inches-by-10-inches in back.

INSET: The 2004 GTO featured a
350-horsepower LS-1 engine lifted
from the Corvette. Sales were slow,
so for 2005 Pontiac installed a
400-horsepower LS6 engine then
under development for the 2006
Corvette. Sales improved, proving
more power is still better.

Pontiac went to General Motors'
Australian division—Holden—for a platform
upon which to create a new GTO.

Because of cost considerations, Pontiac had to retain the basic shape of the Holden Monaro, the car upon which the new GTO was based.

Chrysler reintroduced one of the
original muscle cars in 2004:
the 300C.

One area where the new Challenger pays faithful tribute to the original is in its engine bay. Therein resides an SRT-8 version of Chrysler's 6.2-liter (that's 370-cubic-inches in classic muscle speak) Hemi. This thoroughly modern pushrod V-8 cranks out the same 425 horsepower and 420 ft-lb of torque in the Challenger as it does in the Charger. Unlike the Charger, the Challenger will transmit its power to the rear wheels via a 6-speed manual transmission shifted by a modern interpretation of the classic Hurst pistol-grip shifter. Dodge hasn't released the weight of the new Challenger, but given the claimed performance figures of a 13-second-flat standing quarter mile and a top speed of 174 miles per hour, the engine will be up to the task of motivating the car regardless of what it weighs.

DaimlerChrysler hasn't committed to building this car as of its January 2006 debut, but given the public's overwhelmingly positive response to the car, not building it would be corporate suicide. To grasp the stupidity of not building the new Challenger, imagine that Henry Ford II had not relented and given Don Frey the go ahead to build the original Mustang.

Following a trend towards the resurrection or revitalization of nameplates from the classic muscle car era, Dodge reintroduced the Charger for the 2005 model year.

INSET: Unlike Chargers from the classic era, today's cars have four doors instead of two.

Though some bemoan the new Charger's extra pair of doors, few people argue with the car's performance, especially the SRT-8 option.

One major change in the current muscle car game is that Chevrolet is not a player. With the exception of the sleeper GTO, General Motors itself seems strangely absent from the performance-car world. The failure of the F-cars in a market where the Mustang thrived illustrates the problems General Motors seems to have when it comes to producing performance cars. The accountants running the company repeatedly fail to include one factor in their equations: passion. They cannot seem to understand the passion gearheads that feel for their cars. When asked what cars stirred his passion recently, a Pontiac

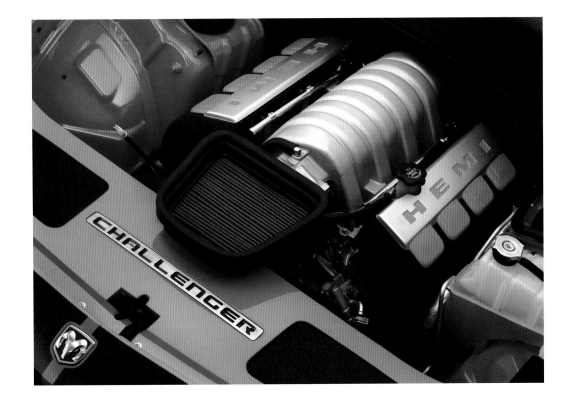

The top engine option for the 2006 Charger is a 6.1-liter Hemi that produces 425 horsepower and 420 ft-lb of torque. This engine is only available on SRT-8 models.

manager did not seem to comprehend teh question. When the question was reformulated to: "What was your favorie car?" he paused, thought about it a bit, and responded, "I had a Beretta in college that I really liked."

If General Motors is forced into bankruptcy, this singular lack of passion will be a primary cause. As something not empirically quantifiable, passion is not easily entered into a spreadsheet. If it doesn't appear on a spreadsheet, it doesn't exist as far as most of GM's top management seem to be concerned. Failing to take enthusiasts' passion into the equation means that the numbers GM's corporate bean counters crunch are less than complete. This could help explain why General Motors' current financial difficulties garner more press than the cars the company builds.

Longtime industry veteran Jim Wangers has seen General Motors' problems coming on for decades. He left MacManus, John & Adams, Pontiac's advertising agency, in the early 1970s, when he first saw the decline coming. "It took GM 35 years to get from the Chevelle SS454 to the supercharged Cobalt," Wangers says, summing up GM's predicament.

The news from GM is not all bad. While Chevrolet doesn't offer a vehicle for the muscle car crowd, the division's Corvette sports car is stronger than ever. It has evolved from the much-maligned "flying dildo" of the early 1980s into one of the world's premier supercars. For 2006, the top performance Corvette model, the Z06, shepherds back one of the most fabled engine displacements of the classic muscle car era: 427 cubic inches. The new

In early 2006 Dodge introduced a new Challenger concept car. Powered by the 6.1-liter SRT8 version of the new Mopar Hemi, this 425-horsepower modern muscle car should burn through the quarter mile in 13 seconds flat. The torquey (420 ft-lb) Hemi transmits its power to the rear wheels via a 6-speed manual transmission shifted by a classic pistol-grip shifter.

427-cubic-inch LS7, with its dry-sump lubrication and aluminum heads and block, represents the ultimate expression of the pushrod V-8. Chevrolet has developed its original small-block concept—lightweight, pushrod, two-valve V-8—into one of the most potent engines of all time. The LS7 generates 505 horsepower and 470 ft-lb of torque, enabling the 3,100-pound Z06 to break into the 11-second bracket. The car can come within a hair of 200 miles per hour if it has enough room to stretch its legs. The new LS7 generates enough power to humiliate even the fabled ZR1.

Unlike the muscle cars of the classic era, all this performance is beyond the means of the average car enthusiast. The 2006 Z06 costs $70,000. Until GM remembers the basic muscle car formula—powerful engine in a stylish rear-wheel-drive car sold at a reasonable price—it is unlikely to connect with the enthusiast market, as Ford has done with its Mustang and Chrysler has done with its resurrected Charger and Challenger. Rumors grow solid that Chevrolet may introduce a new Camaro for 2007, but the corporation's financial problems may cause the division to slide the new car back a year, or unplug it completely.

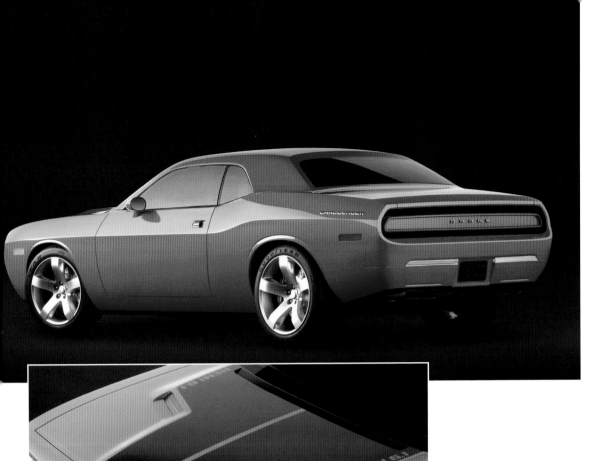

DaimlerChrysler designers managed to retain the Challenger's near-perfect pony-car proportions while giving the car modern aerodynamics. This slippery new Challenger should be good for a top speed of 174 miles per hour, according to Chrysler engineers' calculations.

Even rolling on giant modern rubber (20-inch-by-9-inch up front and 21-inch-by-10-inch in back), the new Challenger retains the look of Chrysler's classic E-body muscle cars.

In 1990, Chevrolet introduced the hottest Corvette since 1970: the ZR1.

INSET: The LT5, an overhead-cam, 32-valve, 375-horsepower, 350-cubic-inch V-8 was the ZR1's most unique feature. The LT5 was designed by Lotus Engineering of Norwich, England and built in Stillwater, Oklahoma, by Mercury Marine.

Regardless of GM's fate, someone will always produce a muscle car type vehicle for the American market. As we enter the latter part of the twenty-first century's first decade, we once again find ourselves in a period of political uncertainty. As was the case in the 1960s, the United States finds itself entangled in an unpopular and controversial war. As was the case in the 1970s, gas prices are soaring and fuel mileage is once again a major selling point in automobile advertising. We may even see the curtailment of high-performance cars, at least for a while, but not forever. "Any crimp the fuel crunch puts on performance cars will be temporary," Jim Wangers says. "Performance cars are the heart of our transportation infrastructure." With over a half-century of experience in the automotive industry, Wangers words carry the weight of authority. As long as Americans have vast expanses of open roads on which to travel, we will have the need for speed. We will also continue to love the great muscle cars of the past. As long as people can remember seeing those cars burning rubber as they drove out of high-school parking lots, the muscle cars from the classic era will continue to define performance, no matter how capable modern cars become. ■

The 2006 Z06 Corvette puts out more power—505 horsepower—than any car from the classic muscle car era.

Today, as always, performance cars are at the heart of America's transportation infrastructure. As long as Americans have vast expanses of open roads on which to travel, we will have a need for speed.

ACKNOWLEDGEMNTS

We are deeply grateful to Jim Wangers, Oceanside, California, retired Pontiac account executive, MacManus, John & Adams, Advertising, for his forward to this book, and for his time, insights, and reminiscences.

We also would like to thank Don Frey, Evanston, Illinois, retired Vice President, North American Product Development, Ford Motor Company; and Carroll Shelby, Bel Air, California, automotive innovator, for generously sharing with us so much of their time, their recollections, and their perspectives.

Further thanks go to the late Zora Arkus-Duntov, and the late Dave Long, for their reminiscences, several years ago, on engine and chassis development at Chevrolet and Chrysler respectively, during this incredible period. In addition, we want to thank Bob Cahill, Jack Cheskaty, Lynn Ferguson, Marvin Hughes, Larry Rathgeb, Gary Romberg, Joel Rosen, and Wayne Scraba for their time and their memories.

Special acknowledgment must go to our good friend and wise counselor Jim Gessner, Mentone, California, who has been part of this project since it was a gleam in our eyes. Jim Gessner's careful attention to our details has helped make this book what it is.

Another good friend helped us in the 23rd hour. We are grateful to fine photographer and writer Mike Mueller for opening his files and providing us images of some of the rarest of these automobiles.

The last chapter of this book would not have been possible without exceptional cooperation from friends and colleagues in the automobile business. In particular, at Daimler-Chrysler, we wish to express our gratitude to Lisa Barrow and Scott Brown, as well as Jim Frenak and the team at FPI studios for the photography of the new Dodge Challenger concept car. We would also like to thank Brandt Rosenbush at the Walter P. Chrysler Museum in Auburn Hills, Michigan. At Ford Motor Company, we are deeply grateful to Sandi Badgett, Jason Camp, John Clinard, John Clor, and Alan Hall. At General Motors, we thank Nancy Libby and Sylvia Paul for their generous help and cooperation.

Several photo locations in this book are well worth mention and particular acknowledgment. In southern California, our friends Robert DeFazio and Doug Stokes at Irwindale Speedway never turned down a request from David to shoot yet another car on, around, or near their track. In Las Vegas, Nevada, Chris Blair and Mark Dawson always welcomed us. These two excellent facilities figure prominently in our efforts to make background-appropriate photographs.

While many owners opened their garages to us, we must single out one great enthusiast for his help and encouragement throughout the production of this book. We are most deeply grateful to Les Quam, Las Vegas, Nevada, for his generous support of all our projects.

In addition, we thank Colin Comer, Milwaukee, Wisconsin, for access to the gorgeous car on our cover.

Producing a book like this requires countless cooperative, patient car owners and car lovers who have opened their collections or introduced us to others who did. We thank Dale Armstrong, Temecula, CA; David Armstrong, Morton Grove, IL; Steve Atwell, Walled Lake, MI; Erik Balzer, Palm Desert, CA; Sean Beardsley, Torrance, CA; Mike Bennington, San Diego, CA; Monty Bernstein, San Gabriel, CA; Cary Bongard, Hesperia, CA; George Boskovich, Camarillo, CA; David Brattain, Whitestown, IN; Christian Briggs, Frico, TX; Lynn Brokaw, San Bernardino, CA; Scott Brown, Oak Park, CA; Virginia and Dennis Byard, Orange, CA; William Campbell, Visalia, CA; Bettina and Otis Chandler, Ojai, CA; Jill and David Christenholz, Scottsdale, AZ; Michelle Christenholz, Scottsdale, AZ; Aaron Davis, Parker, CO; Sam Davis, Woodland Hills, CA; Wayne Davis, Franktown, CO; Bernie DeMarkey, Orange, CA; Dr. Bill Dorset, Duarte, CA; Mark Farrin, Ramona, CA; Katrina and Richard Fleener, Upland, CA; Kenn Funk, Glendale, CA; Robert Genat, Encinitas, CA; Rick Gillespie,

Pasadena, CA; Wanda and Bill Goldberg, Bonsall, CA; Steve Grant, San Pedro, CA; Elvira and Siegfried Grunze, Sylmar, CA; Denny Guest, Matteson, IL; Allen Hall, Allen Park, MI; Steve Haluska, San Diego, CA; Steve Hamilton, Oaklandon, IN; Ronald Hitter, San Juan Capistrano, CA; Mary and Bill Howell, West Jefferson, NC; Glen Hurtado, Cypress, CA; Reid Jensen, Pasadena, CA; Lou Kanellis, Ottawa, IL; Aaron Kanlenberg, Valley Village, CA; Ken Katarynchuk, Calgary, Alberta, Canada; Thomas Kenney, Los Angeles, CA; Rodney Kneece, Bard, CA; Mike Lasky, Los Angeles, CA; Larry Leitman, Tucson, AZ; Jay Lincoln, La Habra, CA; Michael McCafferty, Del Mar, CA; Thomas McKernan, Jr., Costa Mesa, CA; Erika, Matthew, and Morley Mendellson, Rolling Hills, CA; Dick Messer, Director, Petersen Automotive Museum, and Leslie Kendall, Curator, Los Angeles, CA; Bruce Meyer, Beverly Hills, CA; Amos Minter, North Dallas, TX; Linda and Frank Morales, Anaheim, CA; Mark Mosteller, Garden Grove, CA; Bob Neff, Pasadena, CA; Edward Nunez, Burbank, CA; Phil Di Pasquale, Las Vegas, NV; Jeff Paulin, Laguna Niguel, CA; Mark Perleberg, Costa Mesa, CA; Bob Perkins, Juneau, WI; Myron Plotkin, Egg Harbor City, NJ; Gary Price, Hampstead, MD; Harold Schutz, Mount Vernon, IN; Nancy and Dan Smiley, Swartz Creek, MI; Mike Smyth, Albuquerque, NM; Ken Soto, La Mesa, CA; Ralph Straesser, Oceanside, CA; David Sulhan, Allen Park, MI; Joe Van Fleet, Palm Desert, CA; John Varley, Apple Valley, CA; Lloyd Ver Hage, Holland, MI; and Norm Ver Hage, Holland, MI.

Lastly, but most importantly, we are deeply indebted to our wives, who recognize and appreciate that they are the most important passion in our lives. Thanks to Patricia, Carolyn, and Susan for your love and understanding.

Darwin Holmstrom, Crystal, Minnesota
Randy Leffingwell, Santa Barbara, California
David Newhardt, Pasadena, California

All photography in this book is by David Newhardt, except as follows:

Randy Leffingwell: pages 86, 87, 89, 206, 215, 216, 223, 233, 234, 235, 240, 241, 243-top, 274-bottom, 275-top, 285, 287-top, 290, 291, 298, 320, 321, 322, 323, 330, 331, 332-bottom, 333, 336, 343, back cover-top left.

Mike Mueller: pages 58, 74, 75, 80, 83, 92, 93, 128, 129, 168, 172-top, 173, 174, 175, 187, 188, 189, 192, 214, 217, 224, 236, 237-top, 243-bottom, 249, 301, 319, 332-top, 337, 342, 348, 349.

Chrysler Corporation/FPI Studios: pages, 375, 376, 377, back cover-top right.